The Middlepause

The
Middlepause
On Life
After Youth
Marina
Benjamin

Catapult  New York

Published by Catapult
catapult.co

ISBN: 978-1-936787-34-0

Catapult titles are distributed to the trade by
Publishers Group West
Phone: 800-788-3123

Library of Congress Control Number: 2016940488

Printed in the United States of America

9 8 7 6 5 4 3 2 1

in memory of Kirsty Milne (1964–2013)

Look for a long time at what pleases you,
and longer still at what pains you.

—Colette, advising the writer Renée Harmon

Contents

The Middlepause

Prologue

I LIVE ON A SMALL SQUARE IN NORTHEAST LONDON. THE houses—neat, flat-fronted early Victorian terraces—are pretty much standard issue; three stories tall, with sash windows, basement kitchens, and tidy pocket gardens, they were thrown up at speed between 1850 and 1851, when the city was getting fat off the profits of industrialization. The hurry shows. With no foundations the houses cleave together like books crammed along a shelf, each relying on its neighbor to prop it up, and there isn't a wall or a lintel that lies straight. The doorframes all slant and the floors sag: you can't always see it, but roll a marble and it will come to rest in the middle of a room.

I am among those women for whom home is self-defining, as though the house that I inhabit also inhabits me, its spaces, charms, and quirks finding mirrors and echoes in my soul. I like the fact that this home of mine has weathered the years, holding up in spite of its hobbling features. It is how I feel myself these days, now that I am just shy of fifty.

Where I live presently there happens to be a communal garden that has got equally inside me somehow, a triangular-shaped green bang in the middle of the square, that for much of the year is chaotic and overgrown. Its outside edge is ringed with a dozen plane trees that rise out of the ground like giant sentinels and spread their forking branches over the rooftops, while at ground level it is so thickly planted, so dense with branches and thickets, that for months at a time it is impossible from my end of the terrace to discern the outline of the houses opposite.

It took only an instant for me to fall in love with the place. One sultry end-of-day in July 2002, when my husband and I—recently returned from living in the United States and with me six months pregnant—were actively hunting for a home, we rounded the corner into the square and came upon a wall of green, just wild from top to bottom. Blossom-laden trees, blowsy and heavy with perfume, swung drunken limbs out over the road, and unkempt bushes extended prickly offshoots in every direction. I could smell lavender over the bitter edge of the last of the season's roses, and the berries were turning orange on the rowan trees. The profusion of foliage, puffed up like a risen soufflé, was overwhelming.

As we stood there, transfixed, incredulous that such an unruly jungle should have pushed its way up through the brick and concrete, that part of my brain that responds to place lit up, discharging a spray of signals, like fireworks exploding.

A few weeks later one of the houses came up for sale and we pounced. After a couple of months of tense negotiations, and mortgaged to the hilt, we moved in. Local wisdom has it that the plane trees in Wilton Square are the tallest of any residential London street. I believe it.

Over the years we've lived here, I have taken this patch of wild in the middle of London to heart in so many ways, but not least as an emblem and expression of creative abandon. The square is insubordinate and irrepressible—spiky, joyful qualities that invariably get the better of the local council's park wardens, with their leaf blowers and trimmers and mowers. Swallowed up by me, that spiky insubordination is inspirational. When I'm struggling with a piece of work, it spurs me into taking risks, tells me I've nothing to lose. Like a fundamental life force it affirms that to produce is to thrive and that there's a generosity of spirit behind sending things forth into the world: blossoms, leaves, children, books. I feel expansive beside it.

My daughter appears to feel the same way. A few winters back, when everything was flattened and becalmed under snow, she raced outside to make snow angels, gathering young accomplices from the neighboring houses and taking selfies. More recently she adopted a tree. She would disappear into its branches, leaning into the trunk with a book in her lap, and snug there in her leafy nook she'd while away the after-school hours before supper.

Each spring the square is reborn. Children hoot and shout and run amid the budding roses, beds of wild garlic, and snowball bushes. There are dog walkers out early and mothers with strollers benching down for a midday natter. At dusk, groups of adolescents with cheap booze to dispose of meander in, only to be shooed out again by the park wardens arriving to lock the gates. Although for me, nothing beats the heady days of summer, with its tipsy profusion of greenery and merry picnic makers, I'm outnumbered in my household by fools for fall, who cannot get enough of the trees streaked with yellow and russet, as if someone had sneaked out one night and roller-painted them.

It struck me recently that I have spent a full season of my own life here. Moving in, I was six and a half months pregnant, and although not a young mother I was hardy and strong, invigorated by having another life growing inside me. There are photographs of me somewhere, naked and about eight months gone, that I asked my husband to take because I couldn't quite grasp the extent to which my body had been transformed. The photographs were forensic in their intent, like the documentation that accompanies a civil-planning application, when faceless administrators get to decide which expansions and elevations are structurally sound and which aren't. Digging them up now, I remember that I was after an unvarnished, factual record of being fully extended and help-lessly occupied; for there I am against the blank backdrop of the bathroom wall, standing front on, then in profile, and with the belly taking a starring role, because deep down I suspected that this might be my only experience of pregnancy.

So it proved: I am the mother of one child—a girl, now a tween. Twelve and a half years on I barely recognize myself as the same person cataloged in those pictures. I am all hard angles, sagging pouches, and knobby joints. My complexion has become grayish and my hair is lackluster with the buildup of permanent dye. I am past ripe, like those blowsy summer blossoms on the turn, and I'd be lying if I said that I wasn't aggrieved by these changes.

Outside in the square as I write this, it happens to be spring. The cherry trees are starting to bud. The peonies are out. Daffodils wave in the breeze and the sun is shining. With a sorry heave of my chest, I recognize that I have no part of it anymore because the time of my life that was ruled by such cycles, that was attuned to the moon and the tides as to the moods of the seasons, is over. Spring in particular is no longer for me. I am not just out of sync with nature's rhythms, I've got no rhythms. From my study at the top of the house, I check out the young mothers in the square, chatting and gently rocking their strollers. I am glad to have moved on, taken back a portion of my life and released my daughter, now at secondary school, out into the world, like freeing a bird into the skies. But I also feel left behind somehow, the only one who is out of the loop.

Mostly, I am able to shrug off such stillborn thoughts and get on with my life, acknowledging the many good things in it: a tight family, close friendships, my work as a writer and editor (which is as self-defining in its way as the idea of home). But when my defenses are down and I let myself sit with the stagnancy, I sometimes sense at the edge of my consciousness the shade of life beginning to close in on me. This is the world of afternoons and twilights and autumns, and after that, chilling winters and brooding darkness. I tell myself that I'm not ready to be eclipsed.

Hunching over my pregnancy photographs on the laptop, I wonder at the time travel that has occurred. In my head I super-impose the new me onto the old, as if conducting a mental journey in time-lapse imaging. I see the scoliosis that has begun to tell on my spine, gradually crooking my posture to the right; watch my breasts grow heavy, then slowly drop and fall sideways; capture how my smooth, elastic skin has become loose and papery on my upper arms and above my knees. When, I wonder, did the bright veins at the back of my calves start to clump and knot, like soil processed by worms? The years seem to have rolled around so fast. I was thirty-seven when I posed for those pictures, naked and pregnant; now I am forty-nine. Sometimes, but not always, I feel spent.

There is a wonderful series of photographs, dating from 1975 and spanning four decades, that the American photographer Nicholas Nixon took of his wife, Bebe, and her three sisters at their family home in New Canaan, Connecticut, and later in various locations around Massachusetts. The four women, then ranging in age from fifteen to twenty-five, posed together in front of Nixon's tripod-mounted eight-by-ten-inch view camera and allowed themselves to be shot in black and white. Each year, Nixon took a new picture. Some years the Brown sisters glare defiantly at the camera, lips sealed, privacy paramount. Other years they appear softer, as if ready to share themselves with the viewer. The cumulative build of these pictures creates a powerful sense of intimacy. You see these women age by degree. You feel as if you've been watching them for years. They appear to have grown closer over time. Is this an illusion, a function of the photographer's skill, the frame being cropped in? The print tone warming up? Or is it maturity that has worn down the boundaries of the sisters' individualism and strengthened the bonds of care?

What is missing, of course, is the interior story, an account of what it feels like to have gone on this journey, through life, through time, and with everything that this entails: joy and love, grief and loss, rage, hope, regret, and fear. As the years progress, the Brown sisters' faces are etched with experiences about which the photographs cannot speak. Like the presences and absences that you get with brass rubbings, the markings tantalize us with what we'll never know.

I'd like to fill in the silences. I'd like to dig into the gaps between the visible changes that aging inflicts on us all and investigate how the passage of time transforms our sense of ourselves. I could tell you the story behind each of my war wounds, the ones I acquired as opposed to inherited. These are the brass rubbings I would speak of were I to join those young mothers in the square and explain what it is like to find that, without quite realizing where the years went, I stand at the cusp of fifty. My body is my starting point for story-telling, for inducting younger women into the business of getting older. It is also where I feel the need to begin if I am to stand up against the prevailing culture around middle age, which encourages us to disguise it, deny it, and disown it, and if none of that works, to flee from it at full speed until it finally catches up to us and forces a reluctant capitulation. Where such storytelling might go is another matter. It traffics from body to spirit and back again, and also between head and heart. It is my own account of time travel, but its components will be familiar to anyone.

In an ideal world there should be no lesions. No abrupt stoppings and restartings, no gaps or jolts in nature's course. The transition from youth to middle age should be governed by a smoothly unfolding process, like the one seen through Nicholas Nixon's camera lens. Menopause, after all, is a gradual transition. It can last a number of years and work its ways quietly. Women's estrogen levels decline in what feels like measured steps; periods become irregular and unpredictable, and the fuzziness can go on for such a long time it becomes the new norm. When change occurs this way, you absorb it, you adapt. Hair turns gray so gradually as to be imperceptible: one day you'll look in the mirror and be surprised by the shimmer of silver reflected back. Age will have crept up on you the way fine lines do, the way your children are suddenly grown-up, the way your parents seem suddenly old. In an ideal world this experience should feel like continuity.

This is not my story. I entered middle age all at once. There was no real menopausal process, only a Before and After. The war wounds that tell that story are arrayed across my stomach. Four red hatch marks mark the entry points where I had keyhole surgery, and they hover above a reddish slash that looks like a half-cocked smile. It's where surgeons had to make an emergency incision during the hysterectomy I underwent the autumn before last—a procedure that in a mere three hours fast-tracked me into menopause. I am mesmerized by these puncture wounds in part because they're still new and strange, with their silvery alien sheen, but also because they're so tidy; and when I think of all the mess and the blood and the proliferating outgrowths of my faulty womanhood—all the pain it caused me, and all the years I endured that fibroid pain—I cannot believe that my generative organs exited me so smartly, and without the least protest.

You cannot argue with scars. What mine tell me is that one season of my life is definitively over and another begun.

Much of the time I feel mournful, assailed by loss. I wonder if my husband, a couple of years older than me, feels similarly. I survey him from time to time, as objectively as I can. I think he looks good. At fifty-two, he is trim and still virile. He tries to look after himself, goes to the gym, watches his diet, and he gets as much reward out of being a dad as he does from his work (ours is a household of writers). What he mainly feels, he tells me, is a sense of urgency about his productive life potentially running out and there still being so many things he wants to accomplish. How should he choose between projects? And how quickly can he get them done? Unlike me, he doesn't seem traumatized by his fast-disappearing youth, isn't beset by fears of stagnation: headlights locked onto the road ahead, he feels energized, and woe betide any blinking deer in his path.

Although there is no such thing as the andropause—a male equivalent to menopause when testosterone levels rapidly plummet—male testosterone levels do decline steadily with age after about thirty, at a rate of roughly 2 percent a year. Some ebbing of masculine drive, whatever that might mean—fighting spirit, competitiveness, sexual potency—is inevitable. For men, the midlife crisis, if it comes, is less about biology than society. If you manage your life well, you can avoid it. If you can't, then it's time to roll out the clichés: the motorbikes, the younger girlfriends, the fast cars.

Perhaps it is worse for men, who might feel as mournful and outraged in midlife (as shocked by a transition that assigns youth squarely to the past) as women do, and yet have no clear physical culprit to pin it on. Or perhaps not. In my conversations with women, it is the decisiveness and insistence, the importuning, of biology that is the trouble. We had assumed that aging would move over us rather like a desert wind over dunes, bringing about a gentle drift, a shift in shape that would leave our essence, our fundamental "duneness," intact. But for many women it hasn't worked that way. Aging has punched us in the face like a thug and it has been transfiguring.

The unforgiving physiology of menopause can take some of the blame. At one point (or one day, in my case) you are all hormoned up, cycling round the months without especially noticing forward motion, and the next your endocrine system seizes up. The gears and cranks catch and snag, throwing you roughly to the ground. Your instinct is to dust yourself down and try clambering back on, but there's no getting back on the road. No more cycling. For most women I know, this aspect of middle age has felt utterly bewildering. We simply cannot grasp that in the space of a few short years we are no longer where we were and, more disturbingly, no longer *who* we were. We lose our grip on the direction of travel.

In stark physiological terms, menopause represents the kind of enormous shift in bodily morphology and cell function not seen since puberty. It's like some internally explosive chain reaction, triggered when the ovaries, depleted at last of their complement of eggs, lapse into failure, and no amount of endocrine prodding can reinvigorate them. From there it just escalates. With no more eggs to guarantee cyclicity, there is a dramatic fall in levels of estradiol production, while the manufacture of testosterone likewise tapers off to close to zero.

Estradiol is the most important of the body's estrogens. Produced in the ovaries to oversee the business of egg growth and production, it is also responsible for maintaining healthy bones and skin, and for governing the distribution of fat around the body. It has a neuro-protective role in the brain as well, and a hand in improving blood flow in the coronary arteries that encircle the heart. Without estradiol a woman's body effectively goes into a kind of trauma. Multiple symptoms, both long- and short-term, ensue: from hot flashes to wonky and unpredictable fat metabolism, from ovarian atrophy to a loss of bone density. At the same time, the lack of testosterone leads to mood swings and depression, flagging energy levels, and diminishing sex drive. When these changes are precipitated all at once, the anxiety of mounting loss can feel tidal: it floods in and over you, then gnaws away at your sense of self, sucking out your life force.

Though I am now too self-conscious to document the enormous shift in body, mind, and heart in a series of photographs, I nonetheless feel impelled to produce some matter of record. In particular, I wish to bear witness to my sense of being ambushed and laid bare by middle age, in which feeling I know I am not alone. Even among those of my friends for whom menopause has arrived more politely, knocking at the door with hat in hand, biding its time, letting you know that it's there without barging its way in, the blow of finding yourself no longer young has been startling.

"It's more a mental menopause I've been struggling with," one friend told me, "with every significant choice I've ever made suddenly up for review—education, career choice, where to live, children; even your key relationship, which is so established, it requires work." Checkmated by middle age, she is reeling from its audacity, as though nature had suddenly flipped into reverse gear and become hell-bent in the second half of her life on undermining everything she had achieved in the first. When it comes to the "mental menopause," men, of course, are not immune, but they are often more secure in their public roles—their careers, their social standing—than are women in midlife, and so they have a firmer hold on the ground beneath them as the tides of time work at erosion.

When I think about those tides of time and try to visualize the aging process, what comes to mind is Stephen Jay Gould and Niles Eldredge's theory of punctuated equilibrium. It was originally proposed to explain the way that in certain geological periods, the Devonian or Cambrian, for example, you get marked evolutionary "spikes" in the fossil record, representing sudden effusions of biological creativity. Gould and Eldredge looked at the evidence, the proliferation of species represented by those spikes, and concluded that evolution is not a process that unfolds through time with glacial majesty or an even pace. It is more like a form of shock therapy that intrudes on nature's steady state and jump-starts change.

Scaled down to size and fitted to the span of a single lifetime, this is what aging feels like to me. It is a rapid and catastrophic onslaught in which alarming changes bubble forth, unstoppable. What is more, these changes are enacted not around you, but on your very person. Written on the body. As indelible as ink.

Somewhat surprisingly, there are still very few written accounts of what it feels like to be or to become middle-aged. Back in 1970, when Simone de Beauvoir broke ground by writing with scholarly seriousness and emotional candor about the process of aging and society's marginalization of the elderly, she talked of the "conspiracy of silence" surrounding the subject. Four and a half decades on, it is midlife that seems now to be the hush-hush affair. Menopause in particular is still largely undiscussed (except as a joke, which only proves how little our culture wishes to engage with it), to the point where legions of women are not even sure about what happens to their own bodies in menopause, where its causes lie, how long its symptoms last, and most especially what they can expect from life on the other side.

What follows is a personal testimony. It won't resonate with everyone. Much of it applies directly to only half the population, women. But I'm reluctant to get into the kind of hedging that rules out my speaking to anyone outside my specific demographic, since I very much hope that women who are not like me—women who are single, widowed, black, childless, lesbian, disabled—and perhaps even their menfolk, will find plenty of common ground in what I am able to offer. And that is to write about my experience of turning fifty with the same forensic intent with which I asked my husband to photograph me.

I have dedicated this book to my dear friend Kirsty Milne, a kindred spirit and fellow traveler, and a dazzlingly clever and able journalist who was also my confidante, cheerleader, and mensch. Readers who've glanced at the dedication, pausing long enough to do their sums, will have noted that Kirsty never lived to see fifty. She died after a protracted illness, just six months shy of the mark.

Whatever else her loss has meant, it has led me to a new kind of accommodation with my age. How can I fulminate against turning fifty when I am so fundamentally fortunate to be here, vital and intact, when my friend is not? My feeling is not so much one of relief, knowing that my bingo ball is still jumping and jostling in life's pool of contention, and not up, its body surrendered, its number removed. Instead the feeling I'm attempting to conjure is more a lip-biting bittersweetness.

It is not so different from the way one might feel on pausing outdoors to examine a flower blossom on the turn. The outer rims of its petals are darkly tainted and the sepals holding it in shape are wilting from exertion. Soon the flower will fall apart. But still the thing is the more beautiful for being caught between two states; the outlines of its former beauty still intact, it manages, just, to hold its disappearing and full-flowering form—its being and becoming—in perfect tension.

Organs

I HAD ALWAYS ASSUMED THAT WHEN THE TIME CAME I WOULD meet menopause with a certain dignity. Not that the matter could ever have been said to have consumed me. But insofar as menopause presented only a shapeless threat on the distant horizon, it was easy (and also comforting) to entertain a noble vision of my future self, braced for its arrival, my head held high. It would not be welcome, but neither would I regret the stopping up of the bloody purges—more than four hundred of them—that I had endured every twenty-six days, year on year, since I was thirteen and a half. When I looked ahead, I believed I would brave menopause just as I had braved an unusually difficult pregnancy and childbirth that saw me frequently bedridden, twisted up in pain, and several times hospitalized. Compared to that experience, how bad could it be?

As it was, menopause arrived with no preamble, being handed to me by apologetic surgeons like the booby prize in the hospital raffle. The surgeons had excised my uterus, which with its heavy load of fibroids weighed roughly the same as a bag of tangerines, and my ovaries had gone with it in a two-for-one deal. Approaching forty-nine, I found myself barren and in shock. Whatever dignity (if so might be termed the stuffing up of my fear) that I had momentarily mustered to sign the medical waiver lay in tatters around the hospital bed.

Afterward, the surgeons had hovered uncertainly over me, not really knowing what to say other than to admire my wounds. "Everything looks nice and neat," they offered, smiling thinly, their faces blurry under electric lights. (I thought my stomach looked like Frankenstein's monster's.) The more senior of them was wearing a well-cut suit made of quality wool, with a matching buttoned waistcoat, not the usual white coat or surgical greens. I remembered reading somewhere that this bedside apparel was a deliberate signifier, meant to convey to patients and hospital staff alike that the good doctor was on his way out: that he had better places to be. I imagined my surgeon climbing into a slick-looking car and speeding away from the city, accumulating distance on all that suffering as his foot pressed the pedal, and plenty of fresh air to replace the stale stuff in his lungs. But perhaps that was my escape fantasy. The second surgeon, who looked no more than seventeen, was as unhappy as his colleague at having to spend his Saturday morning staring at my punctured stomach. I found myself trying to guess where menopause might reside in his consciousness: young, male, intelligent, probably childless, and with a mother likely younger than me, menopause must have moldered amid the neglected clutter of his mind's unlit basement, somewhere next to stamp collecting and cake decorating.

Their manner was more kindly. "Come back and see us in eight weeks," they said. The words had a pleasant ring, as if they'd really meant them. I made a mental note to the effect that I would have to wait two months before I could start hormone replacement therapy (HRT), and so reassured I sank into an untroubled sleep.

Ever since I can remember, hospitals have given me the creeps. The moment I enter one I start experiencing somatic pain. I have to gird myself before visiting a sick friend or relative, knowing that once I'm inside the building the oncoming wave of sense impressions that together add up to "hospital"—the hothouse lighting, white corridors, the smell of sterilizer cut with the acrid tang of blood—sends shooting pains coursing through my groin, sharp and snaking. It takes all my self-calming powers just to keep on walking. Yet this time it had taken very little to render me docile. My clothes being put away as I readied myself for theater, some kind words, a butterfly-settling premed jab. Briefly, I had experienced a powerful urge to bolt as I stood outside the elevator in my hospital gown and toeless surgery stockings, before being socked by the helpless knowledge that it was too damn late to run.

But that was all done and dusted. My surgeons had given me leave. I was moving on. After just three days, which seemed to have passed in an opiate haze, sleeping and then sleeping some more, the nurses cheerily waved me off to rejoin the ranks of the healthy. The promised follow-up appointment never came. Meanwhile, the world I was returned to was irredeemably changed.

Going into the surgery, I had been somewhat cavalier. I had looked forward to putting behind me a difficult part of my reproductive history. I viewed my uterus and ovaries as an inconvenience, as obstructions that were holding up my go-go life, my work as a writer and editor, my parenting, not least my enjoyable illusions about the tip-top condition of my health. I thought that without them (literally) weighing me down, I could start to move forward more freely: I had even insisted on going in for my operation alone. Coming out of the hospital put paid to all those assumptions.

Menopause is a subtraction, in my case physical as well as hormonal. Organs stop working or are removed and you lose things, youth, luster, vigor, time, most of which you will never get back. A friend of mine, who had expressed concern about how matter-of-fact I was being about my surgery, told me that when her sister had had her hysterectomy she had found it difficult to confront the cupboard full of redundant tampons that awaited her in the bathroom on her return home. No one, least of all she, had thought to remove them. I appreciated the friendly concern, but was so pleased to finally be rid of my unruly organs that in the first flush of relief I set about dispatching any reminders of my own reproductive life with glee. Out went the tampons, the contraceptives, the painkillers, the granny knickers. I would pile subtraction upon subtraction, I thought to myself, remembering that in mathematics when you multiply two negative numbers the result carries a positive value.

For many women, the markers of menopause are not necessarily so easy to see. There will be a slow accrual of subtle depletions that might only register after the fact as belonging to the same transition. Menopause will feel like a slowing down rather than a seizing up, a petering out instead of a full stop: a gentle guiding to your new home, rather than being hurled there by catapult. Perhaps for those women for whom menopause is a process, a staged affair, the jolt comes later: they miss the earthquake but catch the milder aftershock.

Either way, when I look back now, I wish I belonged to their camp, because no sooner had I done the calculus than I realized my error. I'd got the wrong metaphor with mathematics when what I ought to have been working with was chemistry.

Menopause, for me, has been as vivid and as real as the shiny hatch marks carved on my belly that signpost the exit route, and just as implacable. It made increasingly loud demands on top of everything I was already juggling in midlife: full-time work, and then some; sleep-deprived nights, and then some; motherhood, partnering, friendship—and then some. It was a difficult and troublesome presence as opposed to the austere absence I had expected it to be. As I soon discovered, it also had an incredible power to unhinge.

The word *menopause* is derived from the Greek *pausis*, meaning "pause," and *mēn*, meaning "month": "the end of the monthlies." But as the friend who talked to me about her "mental menopause" saw all too clearly, menopause is in many ways more like a rupture, or tear, its sudden precipitation via hysterectomy being only a time-lapse version of an underlying reality, which is that menopause slices lives into Before and After, cordoning off youth from the no longer youthful and forking one's identity into the known self and something strangely other. It is a blunt instrument.

In keeping with this severance, in menopause a woman is forced to negotiate an entirely new psychic terrain, largely in the spirit of alienation. It is an eerie place, spring-trapped with out-of-body experiences and veil-lifting moments that expose jarring, pop-up truths. These, in their turn, are productive of the sort of mood swings and roundabouts not encountered since adolescence, but when experienced in maturity, they lead to a volatile and vertiginous brinkmanship: suddenly you want to pack it all in, give up your job, blow up your marriage, leave the country. You flirt with extremity, skirt around madness. It reminds me of how strong is the pull of the ground when you are looking down from the top of a very tall building.

Every note struck in the land of menopause feels discordant. In fact, the whole thing is like some fairground House of Horrors experience, the only consolation being that once all the ghouls have been sprung on you, and the canned evil laughter has faded, you are delivered at the end of your bumpy ride into an existence of such blandness and monotony (if you believe the rumors) that you almost miss the drama.

A few months after my surgery, I watched a famous soap star being interviewed on daytime television about her hysterectomy and sudden experience of menopause. She had just turned forty-five. It was too soon for her to have to confront her reproductive redundancy, she said. The whole thing had come out of the blue and she was still unspooling from the blow it had dealt her.

The soap star was gorgeous to look at, dewy-skinned, shiny-haired, smiling: physically she was all there. Yet she was also, evidently, in trauma. Sentences would not be formed. Sense eluded her. She babbled incoherently, then paused as if puzzled by where the meaning had gone. Flown from her open mouth. The show's presenters coaxed her gently, but she remained hopelessly tongue-tied. She reddened and flatlined. There was no rescue.

The next day the newspapers expressed concern about her well-being. Was she taking medication? Or perhaps some other, unauthorized, drug? Did she have a mental-health problem? Depression perhaps? Panic attacks? Or generalized anxiety disorder? Certainly, she had a history of instability—which the papers dutifully dug up. Only months earlier, they pointed out, she had fronted an advertising campaign for Weight Watchers: What could be wrong with her now?

I lost track of the story at this point, so I don't know if the soap star rebounded to defend herself against the needling probes. But

I understood her psychic rupture. I lived in a place where sleep was a broken thing, my internal thermostat was bust, my temper kept short-circuiting, and with increasing frequency, coherent sentences would not come. I felt word-choked. Strangulated. I wondered what a shrink would say about the way I kept holding words down. Most irritatingly, nouns, whole families of them, just disappeared. I knew the things I wished to name, which is to say I still recognized objects and understood their utility, but their titles refused to yield themselves even when I stared them down. I birthed a whole nonsense vocabulary. Instead of toasters and schoolbooks and nail clippers and cars and mobile phones and blankets and supermarkets and halloumi cheese, there were houjees and whatsums, bibbly-bobs and thingymenings. My husband and daughter were incredibly patient, gently naming things for me as though I had been newly admitted to a nursing home that they had unwittingly discovered themselves to be in charge of.

If I told you how much warmth would be generated whenever I met a fellow traveler in this new world and we bonded over our shared word blight, you might suppose that menopause had ready compensations. But the reality is more desperate, somehow, like two people clinging to each other while drowning. "Yes, exactly, it's the nouns that go!" a friend agreed in a rush of mutual recognition. But aside from a momentary relief that early-stage dementia might not after all be involved, our parity just seemed to underscore my sense of affliction. Ah, yes, I thought, another soul enters the new world.

On the face of it, disappearing nouns qualify as another subtraction. But what I felt was a palpable confusion. You are aware of the not-having, of straining and foundering and, when the condition persists, of a mounting anxiety. On paper, menopause might be flagged up by a giant minus sign, but in truth it feels more like those test-tube chemical reactions when lithium or sodium pellets are plopped into water and the combination fizzes and sparks, the material zips around manically in an agony of dissolution, and you get Technicolor flames flying in all directions and an irrepressible effervescence of bubbles forming and popping and forming again.

And then it's gone.

One moment you exist entirely within its crazed grip, the next you're ejected, feeling limp and wrung out.

I took a month off work after the hysterectomy, which perversely I had been looking forward to as though it were a holiday. For the whole of the first week I lay in bed, feeling sore and resentful. Over long hours, I struggled to imagine how life might be different—better—once I was up and about. I wondered if I would discover compensating attributes that had been crowded out by my hysterical organs, or experience those unexpected surges of productive energy that fifty-something women write about. More immediately, I tried guesstimating how soon it would be before I could get myself back into the gym. Propped up on pillows, I stared out the window, watching yellow leaves fall from the plane trees and frolic on the wind. Winter looked to be arriving early, and with a retinue of gray clouds that matched my shadow-streaked mood. On the plus side, kindly friends popped in with pastries and offered diverting conversation. It is a measure of how little brainpower I possessed at the time that I cannot recall the substance of what we talked about, only the tonic: walnut brownies, passion-fruit meringues, and strawberry sponges.

In the afternoons my daughter came and sat with me. Flopping onto the bed, she let me futz with her hair while she dished the news from school. She confided that Dorothy had fallen out with Maud, again, and that Miss Harrison had loved her 3-D model of Pandora's box that she had stuck through with drawing pins and decorated with bows, so that it was alluring on the outside but dangerous within. Life, vibrant and fast moving, the way she experienced it, felt like something that took place elsewhere. It blew in with her, so that I caught drafts of it, inhaled its freshness, then it evaporated.

The second week of my recovery I hobbled about the house, testing how far I could push things: Would my stiches strain when I filled the kettle? Could I get in and out of the bath by myself? Then in the third week I was felled by a deep-tissue infection for which I was given gargantuan-strength antibiotics. This translated into another week in bed, most of which I spent reading the kind of books I would otherwise forbid from crossing the threshold of my door. Wellness books.

Wellness is a bizarre publishing category, where self-help bumps up against medicine and flirts with spirituality. You used to find such books housed in the Mind, Body, & Spirit section in large bookstores, but that moniker now feels passé, tainted by 1990s New Agery. Wellness, by contrast is very twenty-first century: no-nonsense, upbeat, feel-good. Wellness is celebratory. And wellness is empowering. Its doyens will tell you that a healthy mind and body are yours for the taking, but that it requires hard work and also the right attitude, a key aspect of which is a determination to turn every negative into a positive. Peer closely enough at any one of midlife's woes or ailments and you will discern in it a coded message semaphoring the need for change. If your bones ache, it is because you are carrying an emotional burden that is weighing you down and that you need to set aside and free yourself from; if you cannot sleep, it is a signal that you need to use your waking hours differently. Every loss is a gain disguised.

Would a good dose of wellness make me well? I didn't know, but reading these books, I felt as though I'd fallen into another portal and stumbled on an underground literature for the initiated, the assumption being that since no one else could possibly have an interest in so dowdy or niche a concern as menopause, it was safe to pack the stuff with hidden explosives. The initiated, meanwhile, are luridly invited in: Are you irritable, experiencing night sweats, loss of libido, irregular periods? Then come this way. . . .

Like some saucer-eyed recruit, I found myself (suitably swaying and delirious) before the high priestess of female self-help, Dr. Christiane Northrup, MD—leading light of the wellness movement, author of a number of books on women's health, certificated ob-gyn surgeon, regular guest on *Oprah*, syndicated columnist, blogger, public speaker, mother, and all-around dynamo. Dr. Northrup is at the forefront of a contemporary wave of wellness-think that sees menopause as a liberation. She wants to reclaim it as a "gift" or blessing, sent to women as a "wake-up call" for them to take charge of their lives, voice their needs, and come out from behind the shadow of being carers, wives, and mothers. The time of cycles, and of cycles of dependency (because, she argues, monthly cycles keep us focused on the needs of others), is over, and a new phase of greater confidence and assertiveness is at hand.

In *The Wisdom of Menopause*, a six-hundred-page doorstop that has been a more-or-less-constant bestseller since it was first published in 2001, she claims that in menopause women's "nervous systems are being, quite literally, rewired" for greater efficiency. "A woman's thoughts, her ability to focus, and the amount of fuel going to the intuitive centers in the temporal lobes of her brain all are plugged into, and affected by, [this new circuitry]." In America alone, she says, 40 million women are undergoing neurological upgrades of this kind, much as if they belonged to sleeper cells in some subterranean anarchist movement that was just now awakening and readying itself to battle society as we know it.

Northrup's message is not just radical but insurrectionary. "We are powerful," she writes, and "potentially dangerous to any institution built upon the status quo." Like "the power plant on a high-speed train," menopausal women will be "whisking the evolution of our entire society along on fast-forward, to places that have yet to be mapped." And the source of this power, according to Northrup? The "volcanic energy" released from the lifting of the "vision-obscuring veil" of women's hormone dependency.

One of the first things that Dr. Northrup put her own volcanic energy to use in was dynamiting her marriage. Like so many women of her generation who embarked on high-powered careers but were still tethered to traditional ideas about being good wives and mothers, Northrup sees family ties as something that hold you back, not up. Only menopause—the stopping of the clock, the calling of time on that cultural reality—lets women reclaim the dreams they might have nurtured before they got fatefully hitched.

Muzzy with antibiotics (on top of that postsurgery feeling, like I'd been beaten up), I sensed that something was deeply wrong with Northrup's argument. But my brain felt addled. I couldn't reason clearly. Momentarily, I'd let myself be carried away by the energy of her writing and a directness that came across as bracing.

Yet even through the fug of recovery something inside me refused her. I could not see how menopause suddenly lets you off the hook, allowing you to write off whole swathes of your reproductive life as some kind of misguided hormone-driven delusion, still less how it might give you leave to behave badly; not so much "I'm menopausal, hear me roar" as "I'm menopausal, now get out of my way!" Northrup, I decided, was too quick and too free with her generalizations.

Among my own circle of acquaintances, I reminded myself, there were a number of women whose marriages, like Northrup's, had not been able to withstand the scrutiny of a midlife perspective. When it became clear that a couple had drifted apart or could no longer survive without the glue of children, grown and flown. Or where one person's dreams had been crushed for so long the person just blew, or else elevated to such heights that their torpedoing was inevitable, and no one, since we're all adults now, was minded to go on pretending. But to lay all this at the door of menopause—more: to see menopause as the "cure"—seemed lopsided. Though I sympathized with Northrup's challenge to redefine herself in middle age and break out of certain culturally imposed shackles, her gunpowder-plot solution just felt too extreme.

Elsewhere in her book, Northrup reprises her insurgent theme more stealthily: through diet and meditation, determined habit-breaking, and sexual experiment, she insists that we can remake ourselves. While working at Women to Women, the women's health center she cofounded in Yarmouth, Maine, she qualified in performing deep facial skin peels. "We did the procedure at the office and then cared for the women at a private home for four days thereafter," she explains. Then, with a linguistic slippage that put me in mind of Aldous Huxley's hatcheries, where bottled babies are incubated in series, she adds, "I always thought of this service as a kind of 'cocoon' experience in which the newly peeled and vulnerable women were kept safe, warm, and healthy while they shed their old skins and prepared to face the world with a renewed countenance."

With their shiny peeled skins and rewired neurons, Northrup's menopausal militants were sounding less appealing by the page; strident, selfish, well-armored creatures I could little identify with. More to the point, if I knew anything at all about my postmenopausal future, I knew that I didn't want to live in a world in which skin peels stood in for rebirth. Tossing the book aside (with a satisfyingly heavy thud), I picked up a volume from the floatier end of the wellness spectrum: *Fifty & Fabulous!* by Jaki Scarcello, a California-based life coach, leadership consultant, and facilitator who claims to have worked with numerous Fortune 500 companies. Scarcello also lectures on something called gerotranscendence, or the process of mentally surmounting the aging process, conceived not so much as a getting over as a getting on top of aging, a mastering rather than a vanquishing. On the face of it, this seemed more promising.

Fifty & Fabulous! is dedicated to uplift. Menopause, Scarcello insists, is "a rich time in a woman's life because we come to these days ripened by the journey that got us here and clear about the fact that we are still learning and that self-knowledge is a lifetime pursuit." Among the qualities women can acquire at this time of life, Scarcello lists resilience, confidence, truth, fullness, leadership, wisdom, passion, skill, success, peace, forgiveness, completeness, risk, compassion, solitude, intuition, vulnerability, talent, and voice.

But since this is not a how-to book, or a medical handbook, or even a book with pretensions to psychological expertise, readers are not offered instruction in how to attain these covetable assets. Only exhortations. In this vein, Scarcello employs an incantatory technique to build rhetorical force and a language that borrows from fairy tale and fable (if you're inclined to be generous toward it) to create a quaint archetype out of menopausal women. Her chosen term is "Women of the Harvest." No doubt she means to invoke by it the idea of doughty workers, scythes in hand, reaping and storing up life's rewards, but to my ear the term carries unfortunate overtones of organ harvesting, as well as vaguely menacing Wiccan intimations. Like something Margaret Atwood might parody.

Scarcello argues that in youth we cannot cultivate ourselves because we are too busy populating our horizons with schemes and plans. But in midlife we recognize that advancing age and increasing freedom, or worldly success (choose your false god), do not necessarily progress in lockstep, and so we turn our gaze backward, cherry-picking what we wish to keep from our life experience as we continue moving forward. In Scarcello's book, this rear-window perspective is entirely benign: there is no mourning of lost opportunities or pining for one's fast-disappearing youth, and there is no existential crisis about aging either, only a bright journey into greater wisdom and well-modulated perspective. As far as I can tell, Scarcello's Women of the Harvest live uniquely for and in the present moment. Like children. "They know that the past cannot be changed and the future cannot be predicted." I wanted to run a mile from them, this fellowship of harvesters who came across as a middle-aged phalanx of smiling Stepford clones.

Northrup and Scarcello offer clear programmatic solutions to a diffuse yet truculent problem, which is presumably part of their appeal. I don't buy their solutions, but many other women clearly do. In their own ways, each author reclaims menopause as something to embrace, not rue. But I wish their message were not simply *you can beat this thing and emerge the stronger for it.* It is a message that appears to have broken loose from the confines of reality TV.

On my sickbed I consumed plenty of other books about midlife, including humorous books that made me want to weep for the individuality they gaily buried amid a mulch of indeterminate crises and haplessly spreading middles. Humorous books are gifted by people who believe that it is indulgent or unseemly or antisocial to dwell on life's problems; people who, though they may be middle-aged themselves, feel that when held up against the outrages of old age, the injustices of midlife are barely worth airing; that midlife's perils and politics are meager and its problems easily solved. Best to draw a veil over the whole business, or better still, laugh it out of court.

There are a handful of intelligent, thoughtful books on midlife. Yet it strikes me that the positive-thinking and self-actualization movement of the past few decades has had such enormous influence on our self-understanding that plenty of writers who ought to know better have succumbed regardless to its easy certainties, its unwillingness to face up to pain, doubt, guilt, fear, or regret, and its damnable good cheer. Admittedly, in the context of positive thinking and esteem-boosting, the shabby business of aging, with its drooping shoulders and drab clothing, must have stood out as being in dire need of a makeover. But I marvel at how common it has become to mistake morale-lifting for genuine empowerment.

And empowerment is now in all the literature on aging, even in its high-end form, where writers with solid feminist pedigrees, such as Angela Neustatter and Anne Karpf, portray midlife's traumas and turbulence as a kind of bad weather system that storms briefly but soon passes, leaving everything refreshed. In its wake there is sunshiny wisdom and patience, life lived at an unhurried pace, gardening, grandchildren, knitting, lots of sage nodding, and not a few encouraging winks to those still cowering under the rain clouds. It proved hard at times in such company to distinguish self-knowledge from self-satisfaction.

It is not that I refuse to believe that something better might lie on the other side of the midlife hurdle, but I cannot accept the idea that weathering midlife's storms requires nothing more than a feisty attitude—hitting up the imagined problem with a one-two punch of fortitude and good humor—any more than I can be persuaded that our messy lives might be neatly mapped onto a 12-step program.

Reentering daily life postrecovery proved to be a strangely muted affair, like stepping out on a snow-shrouded morning when the light is too bright and the sound turned right down so that every action carries minimal reverb. Walking down my local high street, I felt myself displaced, as if I'd been shunted off to one side of things and offered second-class carriage. I moved in the slipstream of the foot traffic, where the shadow people walk— the tired, the run-down, the disillusioned, the lonely—slowly and less purposefully than I used to, and I found myself surprised to be suddenly identifying with people I'd hardly noticed before, people with nowhere to go, or nowhere in a hurry, jobseekers, vagrants, the elderly or dispossessed, not as one bonds with others on account of shared experience, friends, and interests, but on some more abstract level I felt myself to be one with them, part of the mass of undifferentiated humanity, flowing through the capillaries of the city as if without will, pushed along by the collective pressure of others. The sensation was far from unpleasant. It was akin to feeling worn, but accustomed to the ways of the world, exposed and acted upon, but also somehow elemental, like being part of the architecture.

Five weeks after surgery I was still protective of my belly. I hunched over it as I walked, in a kind of mirror image of the way I used to shield my baby mound when pregnant. But my sense of being thus exposed accounted for only part of my new-world experience. The essence of my dissonance lay elsewhere. I felt somehow bifurcated, as if I existed both in time and out of it, and the part of me that felt insubstantial, ghostly, and yet eternal stood slightly apart from the rest, as though separated from the hue and cry by a delicate membrane that allowed me to look in on the action while not being seen myself. Barely visible in the shadowy murk, to one side of events, and alone, I grasped all at once what it meant to be no longer young.

Back at home, I reflected on the experience and the confusion of feelings it had stirred. I admit I felt keenly the sense of my own demotion, a feeling of unjust relegation that sat heavy and lumpen in my gut. But there was also a dawning sense of relief at having been recategorized among the nonvisible; after all, so much of one's life as a woman hinges on being seen, with its attendant pressures of appearing attractive to others and constantly having to work at self-maintenance. Like most women I know, I learned about the defining (and disarming) power of the male gaze when I had been politicized as a feminist in my late teens. Ever after I have danced uneasily around the commodified female world of surface, always wondering what I might appropriate from it and redefine as my own, and what, by contrast, would remain forever contaminated.

This is not to say that the switchblade moment when you suddenly become invisible doesn't pack a punch all its own. It does, and it can wind you. But there are compensations. In consequence of being seen differently, you begin to see differently in turn. Through occupying the same space but with a different status comes the unanticipated freedom of being able to look—and not just to look, but to stare and ogle and glare; to surmise the world around you as you might never have done before; to begin not just to see, but to see through, accruing insight and farsight and, who knows, perhaps even other-sight, by which I mean a kind of laser intuition.

Although these perceptions, both good and bad, still hold, I recognize that I moonwalked through those early days of menopause in semihallucinatory fashion, my light-bodied sensation the result of being utterly and completely sleep starved. I often felt like the test subject in a psychology experiment in which the object of the exercise is to stay awake for as many consecutive hours as is humanly possible. In fact, I had long passed the stage where my nerves were frazzled from exhaustion; I was beyond tired. Listless and slow moving, I felt keenly attuned to the unconscious inner processes of my being: my breathing, my beating heart, the regular rhythmic waves of existence moving inside me as under the waters of a becalmed sea. In this sealed-off state, reality was almost too much to bear. It felt heightened and intrusive, as when the red-eyed test subject, perpetually on the verge of sleep, is repeatedly stung into wakefulness by a zinging electrical prod.

Practically every night since I'd left the hospital I was abruptly woken at clockwork-regular intervals of an hour and a half by an insistent needling, as if a million hot pins were working all over my skin to create a buildup of immense heat. Convinced that I was about to self-combust (and groggily concerned that bursting into flames would endanger my sleeping husband), I would kick off the duvet and run to the bathroom, stripping off en route as fast as I was able. Throwing open the window, I leaned into the chill air to cool off, saluting the moon, like someone deranged. Endlessly repeated, this nighttime ritual proved exhausting, even if the levelheaded observer in me was at the same time strangely thrilled by it, wanting nothing more than to take notes . . . *So, you say you feel like an inferno?*

A month into these night sweats—and the insomnia, word blight, general fatigue, and daily ghost-walking—I marched over to the GP, demanding sleeping pills. She leaned back in her bendy chair, stretching out her long frame like a cat, and purred, "Why don't I just write you a prescription for estrogen instead?" With my assent to that simple suggestion, a whole new psychic adventure began.

Hormones

WHENEVER I THINK ABOUT HORMONE REPLACEMENT THERAPY, the image arises in my mind, ancient, knowing, of the ouroboros, or the snake that eats its own tail. Traditionally a symbol of renewal and of the cyclical nature of time, I've always found it vaguely sinister. Jung, of course, saw in its depiction of self-cannibalization the infant's oral hunger and the nascent ego's inexhaustible greed. And I suppose that when it speaks to me, it says something about a woman's perpetual drive toward self-consumption: the idea that women are so often required to feed off themselves in order to nurture their own growth. Women, as we know, are bound by cycles, and then their cycles end—unwomanizing them in the eyes of some. Except that hormone therapy starts those cycles up again, keeping women fastened to the wheel of life, in homage to the ouroboros.

I suspect there's a parable in this somewhere, about the consequences (and costs) of circularity, of retread. I worry about depletion. I worry that the wells of female emotion will run dry and that the material expense of endless self-consumption is unsustainable. I would like to know if having arrived at a time of life when our bodies no longer regenerate, women might not be better served by simply climbing off the wheel? But this is a submerged concern, buried deep beneath the fraught everyday politics of hormone replacement therapy.

Any decision to take estrogen is political. Several layers of political, with one troweled on top of the next like man-made strata. The topmost layer—visible, public—is effectively a stage on which the whole natural-versus-chemical debate on aging is played out. Picture, if you will, the age-denying Baby Boomer on one side of the ring, baring her peeled skin and newly bleached teeth at Reclaimed Crone, or Woman of the Harvest, or whatever you wish to call her, looking suitably disheveled in the opposite corner, and you have the sum of it. Their fist-shaking tussles over the right way to age are legion, and also well aired in the popular press, while their differences are eternally unresolved.

In this debate it appears that both sides see hormone replacement therapy (HRT) as occupying the soft end of a sliding scale of age-reversal technologies that runs from harmless gels to an array of increasingly artificial, invasive, expensive, painful, and often dubious treatments. Not much truck is given to women who claim that it is possible to plant one's stake in the ground midway along and not slip any farther: you have to pick your corner.

The next political stratum rehashes the *Our Bodies, Ourselves* argument about women taking their health into their own hands and redefining as natural what was once deemed pathological— even if women end up deciding to opt for chemical alleviation of their symptoms regardless. The point is that they (not someone else) decide.

Finally, there is the blunt hammer of misogyny that taints the entire history of HRT, to say nothing of the pharmaco-capitalist-industrial complex that produces the hormones we consume, its profits from sales of conjugated estrogen and its sisterly analogues spinning off into mind-boggling numerals. In 2013, for instance, a Bloomberg report quoted a Pfizer spokeswoman saying the company earned $1.07 billion from sales of Premarin alone. The history of HRT has to some degree been a march toward, if not enlightenment, then at least transparency—about these kinds of nonsense numbers, about clinical trials, health risks, and side effects. But there remain a number of dark and dingy corners to this still-unfolding story into which I feel the need to peer.

My own decision to start taking estrogen followed a spell of creeping around online message boards, reading testimonials posted by thoughtful "end users" and the occasional horror story, too. From these message boards I learned about the virtues of bio-identical estrogen, and of using gels and patches in preference to ingesting pills. Molecularly indistinguishable from the body's own estrogen, bio-identical hormones tick the "natural" box—unlike the more commonly available estrogen analogues, which closely resemble human estrogen but may be more likely to produce unwanted effects (many of them, such as Premarin and Prempro, derived from hormone primers harvested from the urine of pregnant mares). And they tick that box twice over when they're delivered transdermally, directly into the bloodstream, bypassing the liver's structural tweaking.

Bio-identical hormones have an even more pointed political advantage over synthetics. The pharmaceutical companies that manufacture them from soy and yam oils cannot patent them (nature got there first), only the delivery method, notably the glue used to stick the hormone patch to human skin. And I cannot begrudge the pharmaceutical companies their profit on latex if I am getting estradiol for free.

For me, the biggest hurdle in taking estrogen was reckoning with the treatment's desperately misogynistic roots. I felt besmirched by that history, as if by starting a hormone replacement regime I had aligned myself against all women and acceded to the instrumental machinations of the male gynecological establishment: the chemical, after all, is political. But then I reasoned that I, too, could be instrumental. I could take estrogen in the spirit of exploration and investigate what it did to my head as much as my body. Like Timothy Leary taking lab notes on psychotropic drugs, I could report from the field. And I would be rigorous.

But I am getting ahead of myself, since those tainted roots of HRT need to be exhumed before we can move forward—exhumed, and then reburied on fresh terms. Isn't that how we lay to rest the ghosts that vex us?

HRT became wildly popular in the 1960s thanks to the efforts of one man, the British-born gynecologist Robert A. Wilson. Wilson had been in the habit of prescribing large, unregulated doses of synthetic estrogen to menopausal women at his private practice in Brooklyn for years before then, but he was catapulted into becoming America's chief spokesman on the benefits of hormone therapy in 1964 after accepting a "research grant" from the three pharmaceutical companies that dominated the market in female medicine, among them manufacturing Premarin (the conjugated estrogen then made by Wyeth from pregnant mares' urine), Enovid (the first FDA-approved contraceptive pill), and Provera (consisting of progestin, a synthetic progesterone). All the while that Wilson lectured around the country on HRT, loudly denouncing women who chose to age naturally as "castrates," he kept the identity of his paymasters under wraps. Only after Wilson died, in 1981, did his son Ronald confirm the exact nature of the original transaction.

Among these pharmaceutical sponsors, Wyeth in particular kept proffering research and travel grants once it became clear that in Wilson they had found their man: the vehemence of Wilson's message (no longer issued from Brooklyn, but the far smarter address of Park Avenue, Manhattan) and the trembling dread it must have induced in thousands of women who heard his cant and his finger-wagging warnings about not taking HRT made him the fire-and-brimstone preacher of the estrogen industry.

Cannily, given how deeply misogynistic was his message to women, Wilson co-opted his wife, Thelma, as his professional collaborator. Their first joint paper on estrogen therapy appeared in 1963, in the *Journal of the American Geriatrics Society*, under both their names. It was subtitled "A Plea for the Maintenance of Adequate Estrogen from Puberty to the Grave." In it the Wilsons expressed wonder that any of the women they termed "castrates"— those defeminized, brittle-boned, hypertensive depressives, who were content to just "exist rather than live" and to tolerate their "dowager's humps" and the "negativistic" moods, or the "vapid cow-like feeling" caused by "Nature's defeminization"—would resist estrogen therapy once they had been correctly apprised of what it could do.

Estrogen, the couple claimed, lowered blood cholesterol, improved metabolism, retarded atherosclerosis (or hardening of the arteries), and helped maintain bone health, skin health, breast health, and youthful-looking genitalia. So, no more "flabby and atrophic" breasts and no more "thickened, cracked, degenerated" vulvas. What a dream-come-true drug estrogen promised to be, overturning that "cruel trick" played on women by menopause.

To further urge their point, the Wilsons included a couple of photographs of middle-aged women in their journal paper, modestly clothed and hatted and carrying handbags, as typical representatives "of the desexed women found on our streets today. They pass unnoticed and, in turn, notice little." Thumbing through the paper ahead of reading it, I had stopped at these photographs, bemused by the casting of such well-groomed women in a clinical context. If they were meant to be some kind of test specimens, then surely this was a category mistake? One of the women in particular seemed rather stylish, upright, well put together, and confident-looking, with a neat boxy hat, angled with attitude. But it seems my reading was wrong. According to the picture caption, "our streets abound" with such unsexed creatures "walking stiffly in twos and threes" while their "erect" husbands, at seventy-five or thereabouts, can be seen "vigorously striding along on the golf course." The Wilsons believed that women must be educated to avoid this terrible fate, lest they lose their men (and not just to golf, one presumes) as well as their feminine allure.

Three years later, in 1966, Wilson published a bestselling book, *Feminine Forever*, in which he took his lab-grown wisdom to the masses while at the same time delivering a backhanded swipe to Betty Friedan, whose now-classic feminist tract, *The Feminine Mystique*, had appeared not long before. Wilson's book is dedicated to Thelma, whose own early (and risky) modeling of the treatment, or "her capacity to translate theory into reality," as Wilson put it, "served to bring to womankind a priceless gift—the elimination of the menopause, woman's physical, mental, and final emancipation." Thus could Wilson's readers rest assured: it was not patriarchy that oppressed women, but their own biology. Suddenly Thelma was a feminist heroine.

Feminine Forever has been hauled over the coals by many a feminist critic over the years. I have no appetite to do it again in these pages by tripping up Wilson on his own disreputable words. It's too easy. But it is worth noting that even back in the 1960s there were outspoken gynecologists. Johns Hopkins's Edmund Novak (son of HRT pioneer Emil) was one, willing to lock antlers with Big Pharma's relentless and unscrupulous advocacy of HRT. Novak railed against Wilson's pathologizing of the menopause and his predilection for giving elderly women in particular superdoses of potent drugs in an attempt to reverse the effects of aging.

Novak himself was surprisingly in tune with modern sensibilities in favoring the prescribing of low doses of HRT to the roughly 15 percent of menopausal women who experienced severe symptoms, and then only for short periods of time so as to minimize the occurrence of side effects. But he and his Johns Hopkins team were resolutely unpersuaded by Wilson's grandiose claims. Their investigations, based on the autopsies of eighty-five elderly women, did not find any evidence to support the idea that taking estrogen long term could prevent either atherosclerosis or osteoporosis. Besides, asked Novak, "What sixty-year-old woman . . . needs continued menstruation as a 'badge of femininity'?" Quite.

And so my clear-eyed and open-ended experiment with estrogen began. I stuck a transparent plastic patch to my derriere, dosing myself with a drip-drip supply of bio-identical estradiol. By changing the patch twice weekly I would absorb 0.35 milligrams a week. The results were immediate, and astounding. At the risk of sounding like Robert A. Wilson with his lengthy checklist of boons and miraculous reversals, I noticed that my skin glowed and my hair shone. Friends commented on the change, so I wasn't imagining it, plus the night sweats disappeared within days. I had more energy, more optimism, more appetite (for everything), and I am still taking the drug one year on.

Yet its very potency has made me suspicious, as if estrogen's showy personality traits masked some deeper character flaw. The slyness of its marketing troubles me as well. The hormone is billed as a "replacement" therapy, not a "supplement." Which is to say, it merely replenishes depleted stores, topping up your parched system with nothing more than you already had: like a debt repaid, you are entitled to it. However, if menopause is an addition that is generally understood as a subtraction, then estrogen is a subtraction that masquerades as an addition. Its duplicity will have greater traction with women who have not had hysterectomies (which is most women), since HRT generally leads to a resumption of the menstrual cycle. By all appearances, then, it is as if nothing has really changed, as if time has miraculously been added back to the meter on your biological clock.

I admit that to begin with I was so delighted by estrogen's effects that I briefly became evangelical about it, pushing it, like a regular dealer, on friends overcome by fatigue, hot flashes, mood swings, and the rest—friends who, like me, are reeling from how midlife has rudely flung itself at them, exploding like a bag of flour. Taking estrogen, I believed, would hold them steady, as it had me.

However, even I can see that estrogen's staying effect is hallucinogenic. Like taking morphine during labor, the hormone insinuates a dreamy and languorous pause into an otherwise relentless natural process. As long as you're willing to exist within its suspended bubble-like state, it affords you a heightened sense of being at a threshold where you can make conscious decisions about how to tackle aging. It makes me feel as if it is in my power now (at least for as long as I take the drug) to call the shots on how rapidly I am willing to let go of my youth. I am enjoying my revitalized hair and fresh-looking skin, and I am relieved to have regained my vital energies. But should I do anything else? And where should I draw the line? Choice, however illusory, has entered the equation, and with choice comes temptation.

Thus do the glittering therapies at the "hard" end of the age-reversal industry acquire their promising allure, like so many apples dangling from the Tree of Knowledge of Good and Evil. Estrogen has fooled me into feeling younger. So now, in my darkest hours, and by making only a very small leap, I find myself wondering if having surgery on my baggy eyelids will better orient me as I enter my foggy fifties. Or I catch myself thinking there'd be little harm in getting a filler; and besides, who would ever know? I dally with these fantasies the way other women might flirt with the idea of adultery, in that they seem to promise some kind of reconnection to an inner, truer you. It is the siren-like call of the ouroboros, and I try not to heed it even as I find the pressure to look (and behave) young exhausting in its relentlessness.

This ever-present, all-pervasive pressure traps middle-aged women inside a hall of mirrors in which every conceivable cultural image of maintained perfection is continually reflected back at them, and from all angles. Once upon a time it might have been applied by the medical establishment, in league with Big Pharma, but now it is as likely to come from women, and to be peer led. Bombarded with countless images of women who apparently refuse to age, with Madonna and a clutch of frozen-faced movie stars leading the sizable pack, the eye doesn't know where to settle, the mind performs backflips. The images themselves, meanwhile, seem to fuse and separate, then fuse again, so that, practically drunk on them, all you see around you is a kaleidoscopic melee of chiseled bones, pouty lips, globelike breasts, and hair extensions: a collage of body parts and enhancements ranged along the counter like so many consumer delectables. This is the merchandising associated with the new paradigm of middle-agelessness. And it is so much more difficult to resist when one has tasted the fruits of estrogen.

For the first time since I started taking HRT, I make a decision: I won't take estrogen indefinitely. Though many women do, buying the drug privately when the National Health Service refuses to continue prescribing it.

Every now and then I find myself wondering what became of Thelma Wilson, the original guinea pig, tied to the wheel of high-dose synthetic hormones. Thelma: the iconic symbol of age defiance, standing tall (and rejuvenated) by her husband's side as he enjoined tens of thousands of American women to emulate her by signing up to HRT.

On the Internet I trawl local obituaries looking for one that might correspond. I turn up twelve or more potential candidates, a baker's dozen of Thelmas, and I thank heavens for the A that follows Robert that allows me to bin most of them. Several more Thelmas may be further discounted on the grounds of being implausible candidates for the Park Avenue sophisticate who modeled HRT for well-heeled Manhattanites of a certain age.

Then I stumble upon an obituary from The Tampa Tribune. I cannot be sure that this Thelma, who died in Florida in October 2011, and who was predeceased by her husband, Robert A. Wilson, is my Thelma. Following leads from the obituary, the only other information I unearth spirals into the kind of ridiculous detail (itemized court cases, property-buying histories) that the Internet specializes in.

This Tampa Thelma, it turns out, was a registered nurse, who volunteered forty thousand hours at the local Women's Hospital after Robert A. Wilson died. And she maintained a charitable trust in his name. But still I cannot be sure of a match. I know that the original Thelma was a trained nurse, which bodes well, but this date of death, 2011, makes Tampa Thelma an implausibly old candidate: How likely is it that the original Thelma survived into her mid-nineties? So I write to an eminent medical historian in New York in the hope that she might be able to help me. Then, when her leads fail to turn up anything more, I begin to lose heart.

Just as I start to believe that Thelma's fate might have been to simply disappear from history, I come across a research paper written in 2008 for the Center for Justice & Democracy—a civil justice agency in New York. Titled "The Bitterest Pill," it concerns the ins and outs of women litigating over illnesses caused by HRT. But in the midst of the paper's legal recitations, a short section on the history of HRT throws up something unexpected: a reference to an interview that Ronald Wilson (Robert and Thelma's youngest son) gave to New Jersey's *Star-Ledger* in 2002, in which Ronald claims that his father hid evidence that the drugs he foisted on menopausal women were in fact harmful to them. Within a couple of clicks, the paper's online archive obliges me with the full interview.

I had wanted to know the intimate history of Thelma Wilson's relationship with HRT, and whether and when she stopped taking the drugs, especially after two highly publicized separate studies, published in the United States in 1975, suggested strong links between women taking Premarin and women developing endometrial cancer, which had precisely the commercial effect you would expect: sales of Premarin plunged. Endometrial cancer is a nasty thing, usually signposted by irregular vaginal bleeding; but since women taking HRT experience irregular bleeding anyway, they are less likely to spot the pathological kind. It is also a lethal cancer, responsible for more deaths than all other women's cancers except the ovarian kind with which it shares a lack of overt symptomatology.

Did Thelma heed these early warnings, which have grown more clamorous as the years have passed? Did she argue with Robert over the disturbing research findings, or bristle at the super-high doses he was injecting her with? Did she fear for the future of her femininity, which presumably she believed would have been imperiled if she stopped taking HRT?

I wondered, too, how Thelma coped with advancing age as the years drew on and HRT began losing its battle against time. Did she finally surrender to invisibility? Did Thelma ever experience, as I did, the unexpected consolation of walking in life's slipstream among the shadow people? Did she encounter the shock of being displaced—of finding that she was no longer standing where she once stood, in firm command of her own life? Then again, was Thelma Wilson ever really in command of her life? Was she not, like the ouroboros, eating herself up in her quest to stay young? Now that the answers were at my fingertips I felt hesitant.

But I was unprepared for the bombshell of Ronald Wilson's disclosures. Ronald is an animal activist. In 2002, the *Star-Ledger* reporter found him running a pet-sitting service for cats and birds in the picture-perfect small town of Cary, North Carolina. At the time, he owned two cockatiels and a cockatoo, and his house backed onto a retention pond that was home to a rich array of wildlife, including flocks of Canada geese and families of swans. Since the late 1990s, Ronald has campaigned against the abuses of pregnant mares harnessed to the HRT industry to produce Premarin. The mares are made to stand continually in cramped stalls, with rubber tubes attached to their groins day and night; they are kept thirsty to make their urine rich, and as soon as they deliver their foals, they are re-inseminated. These horses are little more than living estrogen-production machines.

In 2002, Ronald Wilson thought that we would soon see the mistreatment of horses put to an end. But he spoke too soon. The abuse of horses, one of HRT's conveniently hidden byways, continues to this day, despite protests by animal activists such as Ronald, and the commitment of a number of passionate single-issue bloggers to disseminate information about the inhumane methods used to harvest conjugated horse hormones.

Ronald Wilson initially trained in the air force, but then spent the better part of his career in radio broadcasting. He is no stranger to the power of the media. Publically, he had always maintained that his father's work never interested him, until the mid-eighties, when questions about who funded Robert A. Wilson's lecture tours and lab work refused to go away. At the time, his mother, it turns out, was battling an aggressive breast cancer, and her illness finally spurred Ronald into lashing out against his dad. Nor was this Thelma's first round with cancer. As she grew dangerously ill, she confided to Ronald that her present illness was a recurrence: she had suffered in secret with breast cancer a decade before, at the height of her husband's lecturing success, when she had also undergone a hush-hush mastectomy.

When Ronald asked Thelma why she had never told him about her breast cancer or mastectomy, she had shrugged her shoulders and said she'd wanted to protect his father's reputation. Now he quipped to the press, "If word ever got out that Dr. Wilson's wife had cancer, there goes the drug." On an equally mercenary note, "he wanted her to be a shining example."

Poor Thelma. She paid an exceptionally high price—too high—to protect her husband: first she sacrificed her breast to his cause, then, in 1988, she lost her battle with cancer entirely. During her final illness, Ronald questioned her about his father's awareness of research findings that linked HRT to cancer, to which Thelma responded, "Dad was not above changing a few facts and figures." The admission sends shivers down my spine, not least because it raises the unsavory possibility that Thelma was a gender traitor—secret party to a medical cover-up that kept women from making informed decisions about their health. Sadly, it is too late to cross-reference Thelma's reported confession with Wilson's original papers: after Wilson died in 1981, Ronald helped Thelma shred them.

I wish that I could somehow unknow Thelma's fate, which, ever since I learned it, haunts me. Far from being the feminine icon her husband wished her to be—for reasons both mercenary and instrumental—she instead symbolizes an entire generation of women thrown to the pharmaceutical dogs for the glorification of men and their industry. Worse still, she might even have been one of those victims who colluded in her own powerlessness, setting her husband's professional standing above her own health, and keeping her mouth shut about his decision to tamper with medical evidence. I want to exorcise her, to lay her troublesome spirit to rest.

In my mind I compose a letter to the younger Thelma. I tell her that I have learned that no woman relinquishes her youth without suffering and that she needs to be brave. (Tactfully, I leave out that it helps to have a supportive partner.) I tell her that taking estrogen might help women acclimatize themselves to the inevitable, but, now as then, it is no elixir. I tell her that today's doctors recommend low doses of HRT merely to cover the menopausal transition, the way a bridging loan is extended to cover debt. After that you have to face up to the fact that the deficit is real.

I tell Thelma that today middle-aged women have a voice and a profile they didn't have when she entered midlife; that plenty of women in their fifties and sixties in politics, business, and the arts are flying the flag for the mature woman and speaking up for her experience and her rights. I tell her that there will always be women who opt for cosmetic fixes, but that there's a roller-coaster quality to that journey that benefits no one. What's more, the brakes are not always within easy reach.

There are many more women, I say, who work hard and retire late, develop new interests and make new friends, achieve recognition or acclaim, win professional respect and coveted awards, and enjoy second or third careers—and marriages. These middle-aged women have made a high art out of balancing work and family commitments.

I tell her that these women live long rewarding lives, keep mentally active, and age healthily.

I tell Thelma, even as part of me recognizes how hard it is to redeem a self-hating woman—and I tell myself.

Looking down the lens at the longer term, I realize that I have been avoiding the question of how long I intend to keep using HRT. I've grown accustomed to it now, to the point where its benefits are becoming less and less palpable. I recognize, too, that I haven't suspended the aging process, not really. I've merely held my finger on the pause button, deferring the moment of my surrender, the moment when I throw the towel in, give up, give in. There's some cowardice in the mix, too, since I know very well that as soon as I stop the drug, the hot flashes and night sweats and depression and mood swings will all return, like some horror-house special sweating it out in the production-house pipeline: *Menopause II*. And right now I just don't feel as though I've got the reserves to wrangle with my symptoms all over again.

Cravenly, I've taken refuge behind the stats. I know that a woman's risk of developing breast cancer while taking HRT is halved if, like me, you no longer possess ovaries, and that while there remains a small risk of suffering a stroke, that number is something like three or four in one hundred thousand, which is a number I can live with.

Yet I am plotting. Somewhere in the back of my mind I am toying with the idea of picking a date in the not-too-distant future, my very own D-day, and when it arrives, I shall simply explode all my residual affiliations to youth. I will be cold and programmatic about it, embracing everything to do with my age in one wide-armed, grabby hold. I will quit HRT, go gray, forgo platform shoes, stop waxing my legs, and sign up for expensive private medical insurance. Then I will dedicate myself to the consolations of being deposed, like the writer Colette, who, upon turning fifty, stoutly declared that henceforth she would devote herself to gluttony, malice, greed, gossip, and the love affairs of others. With each determined step I take away from the world of consequence, I will inhabit myself more fully.

Skin

Since it isn't possible to see the whole of a life, only the part that's been lived, we rely on other people's example to conjure its full potential. We also lean on hypotheses and trick questions. We imagine, for instance, what it might be like to be a decade older, or two decades older, and we strain to visualize what our lives might be like then. More often, we review the lived life, thinking that if we could somehow discern a pattern in its vicissitudes then we might better predict what will follow. Or else we try to identify the high point, convinced that from its lofty stand we will have had the best view of the rest.

Hence the confounding question: If you could stop the clock anywhere, where would it be? Name your pinnacle. Most recently it was my daughter who put the question to me, catching me on the hop. So I told her "now." But that wasn't entirely true. "Before" would have been truer, but only from a purely selfish perspective. Tasked with being more precise, I'm not sure what golden year I would nom-inate. However, I'm pretty sure that if I settled on thirty-five today, it would be forty-three tomorrow and twenty-seven the day after.

Game-playing aside, there are days when I ask myself this question. Not to settle it once and for all, but because I'm tripping. There'll be a wistfulness to my mood and a nostalgic lilt in my heart and I'll lull myself back in sweet memory to a moment I miss, for no other reason than I am inclined that way, that day. I'll twiddle the focus button, the better to savor the sharply defined contours of a time in my life that I was too stupid to recognize as the Best Time. And sometimes I'll chastise myself over it: If only I knew then how good things were. If only I could have lingered. Because you can't know and can't linger explains why the tease has any potency at all. It is a form of sentimental indulgence. But it does toy with the serious point that one cannot apprehend the high-water mark of one's life until it has passed. Like a neglected vintage wine slowly maturing in the cellar, your peak will have come and gone without anyone's noticing. Even you.

Unless something definitive happens to suggest that you might be in decline. Which is what happened to me, and in a defining moment so ordinary that at first I explained it away.

It happened in the middle of the night when I woke up wanting to go to the bathroom. I swung out of bed to stand up in the dark, took a single step in the right direction, then fell to the floor like a plank.

The blunt thud of skull hitting wood and the slap of impact that split open the skin beneath my brow bone, millimeters from my eye, caused my husband no small shock. He leaped out of bed to put the light on, alert as if the crash had been an intruder, and was at my side in a flash. Blood was dripping from my eyelid onto my hand, and the inside of my head was a boom box.

Limping to the bathroom, I propped myself up against the sink, avoiding my reflection in the mirror. I swallowed a couple of pain-killers and cleaned myself up. Back in my bed, I remember lying there, feeling the throb of nascent swellings at my hip and ankle, and thinking, *This is the kind of game-changing fall that happens to old people*—bone-breaking, concussion-inducing—*not to women in their late forties*. I had not yet had my hysterectomy, so there was no post-operative fug I could blame it on. It had to be old age calling to me.

The following morning my whole body ached. Moving stiffly, I made my way downstairs to the kitchen to make coffee, using the wall for a crutch. I felt ridiculously sorry for myself and ridiculously enfee-bled, too. My eye was a billiard ball. Plus with daylight I'd discovered further cuts, also a gouge on the back of my hand where I took the weight of the fall, and where the blood had now curdled into a sticky coin-shaped indentation, like a stigma. None of this proved a deter-rent to getting my caffeine fix. I've heard my husband joke to friends that I could disassemble and reassemble the coffee machine blind-folded, like a soldier putting together a gun before dawn, and I was never more grateful to find that this motor skill had not deserted me.

Over breakfast, my daughter surveyed me from across the table with barely veiled fascination. How was it possible that an eyelid could balloon so much without bursting? Did it hurt very much? I told her I'd had a simple accident. It could happen to anyone. She narrowed her gaze and threw me a slantwise look. In some corner of her mind she was clearly calculating that if I really was that fal-lible (so clumsily, easily, and arbitrarily felled), then how could I continue to be her rock, the thing that stood like a seawall between her and the dangerous churn of the world.

As we sat there together, my daughter appraising me in new and unexpected ways, I felt myself slide from an unchallenged place in her estimation where I had previously enjoyed the firmest of footings. As if literally falling were not humiliation enough, I had to endure a symbolic taking down. Not wanting to think too hard about this, I dismissed the fall as a simple case of somnambulism and got on with things.

Looking back, I believe that it registered much deeper, leaving me feeling that the open pathways of my nervous system (busy translating conscious intent into motor action) had been ambushed by rogue forces. On this reading, my fall fit with a view of the world I've never consciously subscribed to, that pictures higher beings or godly powers meddling in human lives and that casts poor mortals as players or marionettes, beholden to the whims of unseen string-pullers, or as flimsy vessels they might set adrift on choppy seas. The more I thought about my fall, the more portent-like it seemed. It was an object lesson, a warning, a sign. Like some bizarre prefiguring of my future life, it seemed to contain within it the seed of every other fall I would henceforward suffer. In a sudden moment of clear-sightedness, I saw a future unfold before me along a path strewn with props I wanted nothing to do with—walking sticks, crutches, braces, wheelchairs.

I am not alone in feeling as if falling somehow foreshadows a state of collapse. After I wrote an article about my nighttime adventure, women I knew (and some I didn't) e-mailed and tweeted me about it. They, too, had been blindsided after taking a fall, their sense of competence unexpectedly and egregiously undermined. One wrote, "It seems as if middle-aged women falling is a *thing*." I had the clear impression that for many women the looming threat of their own redundancy and a fear of falling had become worryingly entwined. Falling, failing . . . just one letter separates them. The link wasn't always there.

When the term *middle age* came into general use in the late nineteenth century, it was principally in a socioeconomic setting. Empire and industrialization had expanded and enriched the middle classes on both sides of the Atlantic, and this, coupled with a demographic trend for having fewer children, meant that women who'd finished raising families were able to enjoy another decade or two of vigor and relevance, while the relatively small number of educated women who worked could stop. (Among working women with no option to stop, middle age was not considered a hindrance, if it was considered at all.) Middle age was admired: these women were mature, worldly beings, having, as the modern saying goes, "freedom to" as well as "freedom from." In an essay published in *Cosmopolitan* magazine (ever the arbiter of fashions in femininity) in 1903, "The Woman of Fifty" was hailed as someone who had attained a "mastery of the rules" of life. She was characterized as having "distinctive charm and beauty, ripe views, disciplined intellect, [and] cultivated and manifold gifts."

This perception of womanly self-possession went hand in hand with an expansion of women's rights. In the UK married women obtained new authority and respect through the Married Women's Property Acts of 1870 and 1882, which entitled them to divorce and to hold property and wealth, while suffragettes pushing for electoral reform were in 1918 rewarded with the vote. This is well known; less well known, perhaps, is that prior to 1918, widows who owned property could vote in local elections. Widowhood was, of course, freeing in other ways, offering such compensations for personal loss as allowing women to embark on philanthropic careers, or to devote themselves to charities, good works, or the causes of reform; as Sylvia Townsend Warner's redoubtable heroine Lolly Willowes, a woman who chooses spinsterhood over marriage so as to ring-fence her freedom, remarks, "Nothing is impracticable for a single, middle-aged woman with an income of her own." Midlife's negative tarnish came only with the advent of mass production in the 1920s, and the theories of "scientific management" that underpinned it, sharpening our association of youth with productivity, and middle age with decreasing efficiency.

Scientific management was the brainchild of American engineer Frederick Winslow Taylor. While working as a foreman at a Philadelphia steelworks, Taylor began studying the human component of the production process as part of his search for ways to enhance worker efficiency. Quickly he saw that if workers might be given specialized, routinized, and highly circumscribed roles—in other words, if they could somehow be made to behave more like machines—then the production process might be streamlined and redundancy obviated. Taylor's *Principles of Scientific Management* was published in 1911, swiftly becoming the bible of mass produc tion, with Henry Ford its greatest champion. Under Taylor's influence, Ford managed to cut the time it took workers to assemble a car at his Detroit plant from twelve and a half hours in 1913 to just an hour and a half a year later, by breaking down the chain of production into ever smaller component parts, all of them amenable to rapid repetition.

In the Taylorized system, time was of the essence as never before. "Speedy Taylor," as he soon became popularly known, believed every second counted. From the minute workers clocked in to the moment they clocked off, their managers were to remind them they were as much a part of the production line as the cogs and wheels and levers and gears that pumped and oiled the machinery on the factory floor.

Yet it wasn't just manufacturing that could be made more efficient on the Taylorized system. As Speedy himself argued, "The same principles can be applied with equal force to all social activities: to the management of our homes; the management of our farms; the management of the business of our tradesmen, large and small; of our churches, our philanthropic institutions, our universities, and our governmental departments." All of life might be Taylorized.

In this by-the-numbers vision of progress, human life itself might be broken down into a series of successive standardized stages, from childhood and adolescence, through adulthood, middle age, and finally senescence, at just one phonetic skip and hop from obsolescence—the bête noire of Taylorism. These stages mapped the rise and fall of productivity, but critically, they could also be measured. As Patricia Cohen observes in her wide-ranging study of midlife, *In Our Prime: The Invention of Middle Age* (2012), age became "a proxy for efficiency." Cohen charts how the spread of Taylorism led to a sea change in the way midlife was viewed that showed itself not only in sweeping pronouncements made by doctors, sociologists, and psychologists, but in the little ways that ordinary people behaved as well: rounding down their age for census questionnaires, as opposed to rounding up as they once did, and acting on a decided reluctance to go gray: sales of hair dyes shot up in the 1920s and '30s.

Edith Wharton's 1927 novel, *Twilight Sleep*, portrays just such a middle-aged woman, caught up in these cultural cross-wires and determined to maintain appearances at all costs. Pauline Manford is beset by Machine Age anxieties about breakdown and redundancy, and she meets them with a Taylorized fury for superefficiency that speaks to the modern working woman with uncanny accuracy. Her daily regime is a procession of tightly packed improving activities interspersed with do-gooding: "7.30 Mental uplift. 7.45 Breakfast. 8. Psycho-analysis. 8.15 See cook. 8.30 Silent Meditation. 8.45 Facial massage. 9. Man with Persian miniatures. 9.15 Correspondence. 9.30 Manicure. 9.45 Eurythmic exercises. 10. Hair waved. 10.15 Sit for bust. 10.30 Receive Mother's Day deputation."

Though moneyed and enviably established socially, Pauline comes from a trade background. When she married Arthur Wyant and entered the ranks of Old New York society, she was "fresh from the factory-smoke of Exploit"—her father's motor manufacturing business. Presumably it was there she imbibed the principles of Taylorism she lives by, much as she lives by (should Taylor's system fail her) the hip-slimming eurythmic exercises, or "holy ecstasy," taught by "the Mahatma" at his School of Oriental Thought— clearly the Bikram yoga center of its day. Wharton writes that Pauline could make "loveliness and poetry sound like the attributes of an advanced industrialism, and babies something to be turned out in series like Fords." She is, if you like, the line manager of her own personal evolution.

When we meet Pauline, she is in the throes of a midlife crisis, although she herself is unaware of the fact. Lita, the beautiful wife of her son Jim Wyant, is threatening divorce; Pauline's daughter Nona, from her second marriage, to society lawyer Dexter Manford, is unhappy, and worse, unmarried; and Dexter himself is strangely distanced from her, bored with her glittering parties, and dangerously attracted to Lita.

In the face of these problems, Pauline's solution is to "think them away" by throwing herself into the endless round of do-gooding that mops up whatever slack remains in her hectic schedule. But when Pauline finds herself struggling to manage her errant family, Wharton puts her case more plaintively: "What was the use of all the months and years of patient Taylorized effort against the natural human fate: against anxiety, sorrow, old age— if their menace was to reappear whenever events slipped from her control?"

When *Twilight Sleep* first appeared, it was widely castigated as heavy-handed pastiche. Wharton was in her sixties when she wrote it, living abroad in France and desperately out of touch with modern American life, or so her critics averred. Along with her other Jazz Age novels, *Twilight Sleep* was dismissed as unequal to her earlier masterworks. Yet beneath the novel's domestic melodrama lies a searching examination of a society in thrall to modern science and commerce, convinced that between them might be found the panacea that would cure all of humanity's ills—anxiety, sorrow, and old age chief among them.

Wharton followed developments in modern science with keen interest. She considered Charles Darwin and Herbert Spencer to be among her most "formative influences," and she scribbled energetic and incisive annotations in the margins of books in her library: Thomas Huxley on evolution, George Romanes's philosophy, Edvard Westermarck's anthropological studies. But as Cheryl Miller notes in an essay for *The New Atlantis*, by the 1920s Wharton had begun to question the aims and ethical underpinnings of modern science, especially its ambition to relieve people of pain and suffering. Over in France she collected myriad news clippings and advertisements from home, announcing the latest scientific breakthroughs and fads, whose empty promises would become fodder for her satire. She was deeply mistrustful of the world she placed Pauline into, "a world which believed in panaceas."

Nowhere is the sterility of scientific self-improvement more clearly shown up than in Pauline's high-tech bathroom, a pristine sanctum of rejuvenation that "looked like a biological laboratory, with its white tiles, polished pipes, weighing machines, mysterious appliances for douches, gymnastics and 'physical culture.'" Again, the modernity of this environment—half clinic, half consumer heaven—is striking, and I can't help thinking how that army of twenty-first-century Paulines, sold a bill of goods by the multi-billion-pound cosmetic, pharmaceutical, and surgical industries, would wholeheartedly approve. Mercifully, the reader is spared the unhappy rigors Pauline puts herself through in that cold, hard room as she tries to "de-microbe life" and "whitewash" pain. Though Wharton is quite plain that these efforts are of little avail.

Reading the novel today carries an added edge for me, since pinning down and explaining, even laughing off, the anxieties of midlife doesn't make them go away. In spite of its comedy, *Twilight Sleep* holds many poignant moments—one of the most stinging being when Pauline fails to reanimate the interest of her straying husband. She has won a prized dinner invitation from a family that has snubbed her since she divorced Wyant and is buzzing with excitement at the prospect of restitution. But when Dexter begs her to cancel the engagement, saying he wants to spend the evening alone with her, Pauline gladly complies. She dresses carefully for their assignation, daring to hope for the kind of romance her diary-keeping, line-manager self would dismiss as "nonsense" in a woman her age. In the event, however, Dexter desires Pauline's undivided attention only to avail himself of his concern for Lita.

He spends the entire evening outlining a plan to rescue Lita from herself and stop her from walking out on her marriage to Jim.

At the end of this demoralizing evening, once Dexter has excused himself and gone to bed (without remembering to say good night to his wife), Pauline takes stock. She reorders the furniture so that it looks as it did before Dexter disturbed it, then she "attentively scrutinized" herself in the mirror. The light is "unbecoming," so Pauline adjusts it. But still it's no good. What ought she to expect from her reflection, she tells herself, after such a day. She mouths her familiar mantra: "Pauline, don't worry: there's nothing in the world to worry about." But the image in the glass refuses to soften: "The rouge had vanished from the lips, their thin line looked blue and arid." Pauline turns from this unpleasing sight, putting out light after light as she makes her way to her dressing room, and the separate beds of her marriage—each light snuffed out symbolizing another corner of her life over which darkness is falling. Here, then, is the end of youth, the end of love, and, also, the end of hope.

This is a long way for any woman to fall. To be wrong-footed by taken-for-granted assumptions. To trip up over what is familiar and trusted. To find that the ground beneath your feet has shifted, and the place you thought secure, and upon which you had built the supposedly enduring structures of your world—home, marriage, career, self-worth—in fact straddles a dangerous fault line. These breakthrough truths (epiphanies, revelations, call them what you will) that falling brings to light disrupt one's fundamental sense of what is real. They crack the surface calm and throw up jagged edges, often along fissures we will have spent decades attempting to disguise or hide from, and they show up the fictions we impose on passing time for what they really are: fictions of continuity.

The title of Wharton's novel, *Twilight Sleep*, refers to the semi-anesthetized state produced by the mixture of morphine and scopolamine that was given to women during childbirth to help them forget their labor pain. However, Wharton clearly meant to imply that the anesthetic solutions of modern science, with which Pauline Manford medicates her own pain, have induced a more dangerous kind of forgetting. To underline the point, Wharton's cast of moderns who believe themselves to be beyond superstition, thanks to America's enlightened progress (thanks to plumbing, dentistry, and easy divorce), are undone by the same old human problems: overreaching, selfishness, infidelity—things that proved as impossible to leave behind in the Old World as sorrow and superstition. In the novel Lita is the agent of this undoing, and her threat to Pauline is embodied by her youth.

Lita is youth personified, the new series model, and she is everything that Pauline is not—lazy, torpid, slow moving. Where Pauline is perpetually giving of her energies, Lita depletes the energies of others. Her boudoir is black, and she its still center, a black hole, greedily consuming all the light. Lita couldn't care less for the good opinion of others: she'd much rather scandalize them. Although Wharton implies that notoriety is the most that someone like Lita might achieve, she does make her beautiful. She gives her pale luminous skin, a heart-shaped face (made for loving), and "goldfish-colored" hair. And she makes her tall and willowy, whereas Pauline, though elegant, and in possession of nicely turned ankles, has a steady build: Pauline "sweeps," while Lita "floats." Lita is painted as a delicate flower, an exotic hothouse creature. Wharton makes repeated reference to Lita's decorative hands, unfitted for any kind of labor, Taylorized or not: Lita's hands are perpetually upturned, or they trail through the air like tendrils.

Against such an opponent as Lita, with youth *and* beauty in her arsenal, a woman like Pauline doesn't stand a chance.

When I first read *Twilight Sleep*, many years ago, in the initial flush of my independence, when I thought myself indestructible and felt the early intimations of my own sexual power, it was Lita who shone out for me. Her flapper's nonchalance and her commitment to "expressing her personality" felt incendiary. When she danced, she emptied the floor; when she entered a room, she commanded its attention. It was as if she could freeze-frame time itself. Now it is Pauline for whom I feel a sympathetic attraction, as might any woman who in middle age feels herself endangered, not simply past her prime, but on the verge of being eclipsed by the next generation.

The Machine Age anxieties that Wharton diagnosed in 1927 are still very much with us. Although in developed parts of the world we now live in a postindustrial society, we continue to be enslaved by the habits of Taylorism. We are as mindful now of how and where we occupy our time as ever we were—perhaps more so, since the newer, more fluid ways of working enabled by increased connectivity have meant that the production line follows us home long after we officially clock off. We are seldom not working. For women who are breadwinners, this perpetual employment chafes against other, equally deserving commitments: aging parents, growing children, the restorative pull of rest and leisure. In fact, the older you are as a working woman, the more you need to work, if only to prove that you remain on the right side of redundancy.

This is where the quackery of antiaging heaves into view, with all its medicalized paraphernalia lit up like some alien spaceship;

its superlative claims and hype-stuffed promises; its white-coated assurances, shiny miracle creams, and invisible fillers; its surgical lifts and endocrine boosts—all of it in the service of unstitching time. Its purpose, of course, is to reassure. To tell us that we need not relinquish youth just yet. That there are ways of stalling our foe, and with results that are clearly visible, at the very least on our skins—and in a culture obsessed with surface, that hardly counts as a drawback.

In the introduction to my Virago edition of *Twilight Sleep*, Penelope Farmer underlines Edith Wharton's extensive use of mirrors and clocks as stand-ins for female anxiety. Pauline lives by them both. She is perpetually marking, beating, and consuming time, terrified to take her eye off the clock in case time devours her first. And she is forever checking her progress against this enemy, time; assessing her finely lined features in the looking glass, or wondering if her hips are sufficiently reduced and her ankles still slim. As Farmer puts it, "Pauline is always seeking reflected assurance that she is still overcoming time."

Again, the striking contrast is with Lita, who is also fixated on her mirror reflection but prefers to "keep on finding herself, immeasurably magnified, in every pair of eyes she met!" Lita, as you might guess, is cavalier about passing time. At the Manfords' country estate, where "all the clocks agreed to a second," she moans that "one could never believe them." She thinks "they must have stopped together, twelve hours before." Besides, she asks, "What's the use of knowing what time it is in the country. Time for *what*?"

I long for the days when time lay that heavily on my hands. When I spent hours in my student digs, lolling; or later, when busy workdays and social weekends were accorded their proper stretch, and the calendar stuck to the wall seemed full of endlessly movable feasts rather than looming deadlines and birthdays I'd rather not have. I am all too painfully aware now of how fraught is a middle-aged woman's relationship with time, with watching the clock but not wanting to mind it; and equally sensible of the push and pull of wishing yet not wishing to see my reflection in the mirror, which instrument, after all, is the measure of how well I am doing against all those clocked-up months and years.

I have always felt uneasy around mirrors. Even when there was nothing to scare me about what might be reflected back, I threw up barriers against them. When you are young, a mirror is not so much a tool for self-inspection as it is a window onto a series of potential yous. It is a performative aid, at once amplifying and forgiving. I certainly paid my dues before the mirror; costumed and playful, I would stroll up to the giant oracular circle of my bedroom mirror, walk away, then turn my head to view myself from behind, trying on different personae as though they were sharp new items of fashionable clothing. If I judged that some way of moving or being suited me, I adopted it. If it didn't, out it went. And yet (another performance?) I have kept a photograph of myself that I took when I was about sixteen, in which I'm facing my bedroom mirror square on so that where my face ought to be you see a camera lens instead. That I've kept the picture at all is a determined reminder of how much I desired, even then, when looking at myself was generally pleasing, to be the seer and not the seen.

Lately I've been approaching mirrors with renewed trepidation. Largely this is a learned response, since any chance encounter with a mirror delivers a momentary jolt, born of a millisecond's conviction that no one I recognize is staring back. So I adopt guises. Mostly I'm an invigilator. I police my features for signs of decay, prodding my cheeks to test spring-back, scanning for general puffiness, haggard-looking eyes, drooping lids, fine lines, deep furrows, burst capillaries, and whiskery hairs. Other times I'm a supplicant, determined to intercede against the weight of the evidence. I adjust the light, force a smile, and tell myself that all is not lost, that with some good moisturizer and foundation I can be fixed up to look almost as good as before. At my most morbid, I'm an accountant, opening up the ledger books to record the latest gains against my losses, a graying temple for a softer curve of the cheek, a new wrinkle for a better haircut. The accountant holds out little hope, since the ledgers cannot be balanced forever: in a year or two they're going to register a net loss, and after a few more years of dreadful deficit there'll be nothing left but to begin foreclosure.

. This accountant has become a regular fixture in my life, calibrating every opportunity that arises or is shut down against what time is left. On the plus side it can generate a sense of urgency and momentum around what I want to do or achieve, and embolden me to say no to commitments that threaten to bog me down. But this continual accounting is also wearying. It's as if I've forgotten how to be free. My husband detests this accountant. "You always used to be up for an adventure," he tells me whenever I ring a note of caution or find excuses to not join him in some off-piste scheme or impulse. "What happened?" It makes my heart sink, since I long to reach out to the younger, carefree me, and reabsorb her into my being, to revivify myself with her life force while the accountant tut-tuts behind my shoulder.

When it comes to the mirror, however, the accountant wins. It is a well-documented fact that we humans possess acute powers of facial recognition, a specialization that has been located in the amygdala and also an area in the temporal lobe known as the fusiform gyrus. Inside the libraries of the human brain we store many thousands of unique configurations of facial features that allow us to identify people we've only had the briefest encounter with, as well as people we've known well but not seen in decades. It is thought that the brain constructs an internal 3-D memory model of an individual's face so we can identify the person from different angles.

All of which makes me wonder if this talent isn't what makes our self-scrutiny in midlife so disconcerting. Is it because we have cataloged in our minds exactly how we once looked that we are perpetually shocked when we fail to see our "true selves" reflected in our middle-aged faces? And does this same capacity to log granular distinctions in a face mean that we notice every tiny degradation and slippage, as if our neural networks were our very own time-lapse cameras?

This is murky territory, where cognition blurs with social programming. After all, human perception is forever playing tricks with time. When we're afraid, time slows down, so that every minute that passes feels like a small eternity. Likewise when we're stuck in a queue, or waiting for a bus to arrive or the phone to ring. Conversely, when the going is good, time speeds up. Who hasn't arrived at the end of an exciting few weeks of travel, for example, only to feel as if it's all been a whirlwind?

Time also feels as if it is accelerating the older you get. In *Time Warped* (2012) the British social psychologist Claudia Hammond discounts the idea that some objective measure of perception is in play here that makes sixty-year-olds, say, feel as if time is moving exactly twice as fast as it did when they were thirty. Instead she suggests we might be responding to an increase in *tempo*. This implies that the more experiential mileage we squeeze out of any given day or week or year, the faster it seems to fly.

There are also studies that show that the greater a person's age, the more rapidly they will say the previous decade elapsed, a phenomenon that Hammond believes has to do with autobiographical memory. This makes sense to me, since the older you get, the more you notice the recurrence of things you've come across before—novels that recast familiar plots, songs that recycle past hits, fashions that return over and over. A mature decade stuffed in this way, with repeat experiences, will feel faster than a decade experienced in youth, when so much of what you come across is novel. Another, related form of telescoping says that the more impact certain experiences have had on your life, the more magnified they are in memory, and consequently the more recent they feel.

I wonder if this telescoping argument can be made to pay forward? By which I mean, I wonder if the landmark moments that are magnified on our horizons because we anticipate them keenly, whether with joy or dread, loom similarly large in our minds—on which reckoning they would surely feel as if they were rushing toward us? This is how I feel about turning fifty.

So much so, that if you made me play "stop the clock," I'd dig my heels in determinedly at forty-nine and ask to get off, like a child at a fairground ride that was turning out to be faster and rougher than bargained for.

Against this backdrop, the inner wheels in my mind churning depressingly over my upcoming milestone birthday, my family is pressing me to celebrate. Throw a party. Do something wild. Mark the damn thing and own it, they cry. I'm tempted. Sometimes. But for whatever reason, fifty feels different to thresholds past. It feels tarnished as an old coin, and worn—worn down and worn out. And fifty feels heavy at some elemental level, as if dense with neutrons. There is nothing at all glamorous about fifty that I can see, not even in some retro way, since fifty feels like my mum. But then I think of my counsel to Thelma Wilson, and I'm minded to do something after all.

My husband, who is American, has acquainted me with a well-worn US joke made at the expense of anyone who is about to turn fifty. A few days before their birthday US citizens will reliably receive a welcome pack from the American Association of Retired Persons, wishing them a happy half century and supplying them with a load of advisory bumf about pension plans and life insurance policies, retirement schemes and solo holiday deals for the newly widowed. The joke is grim: as my husband's mother put it when she was about to turn fifty and experienced the future rushing toward her, "I suppose AARP will be sending me my death warrant."

In England, barely twenty-five years later, a different kind of postal assault lies in wait for women who are about to turn fifty. In the months ahead of my birthday I've been the bewildered recipient of a variety of catalogs promoting expensive skin-care treatments for aging skin: deep-cleansing oils and antiwrinkle creams, and serums "enriched" with enzymes, collagen, and other suspicious "bioactive" ingredients. And, reader, I have bought some!

At the same time, I have been targeted by lingerie companies whose catalogs are full of not-so-skimpy, wire-girded armature, in candy colors. These catalogs give me my riposte to the American joke: not the death warrant, but the rejuvenation pack. Once again, the mirror is entangled with the clock, except this time the crazy promise is that somehow, with the magic tools of rejuvenation, you can spin the dial backward. Oh, to be young (*juvenis*) again (*re*) . . . This is not just self-preservation, not just maintenance and upkeep, but full-bodied overhaul. Its allure is undeniable.

But there is a double bind at stake here—one of many that tie middle-aged women up in knots. For any relentless attempt to beat time at its own game, by moving fast enough to outstrip it, or indeed fast enough to send it, in Einsteinian fashion, into reverse gear—by taking hormones, for example, or having little nips and tucks—and thus emptying time of its power to alter things, is doomed to failure. And yet slowing down, falling, taking stock: these are the enemies of the middle-aged woman, as well, because at those moments when you stop long enough to assess where you are, you come into the full inheritance of aging, which, in turn, gives the lie to the hubristic idea that anyone is capable of mastering time in the first place. We cannot. We don't. As Pauline Manford knew at her core (which is why she fought it so hard), time passes and it passes us by, without a single rearview glance in our direction.

Muscle

"So short!" Just two declamatory words. They were among my father's last, uttered when his speech had become a series of staccato pronouncements ("Water," "Get Mum," "So tired"). Islanded on a hospital bed equipped with sophisticated medicinal pumps, an oxygen tank, electric UP and DOWN touch pads, a catheter bag, and inflatable leg supports, my father spent his last weeks completely immobilized by lifesaving devices.

Though he was far from a passive presence. He twitched and fidgeted, and occasionally he shouted out in protest or pain, or anger, or the sheer frustration of not being able to move; we couldn't tell, and he couldn't elaborate. But the smallest of his actions went a very long way, exerting an almost magnetic pull. It was as if an emotional tempest swirled within and around him at all times, sucking in everything within reach—family, nurses, doctors, friends: "Come," he'd call to whoever walked past, before enlisting them.

The ungainly bed-island was marooned in the daylong dark of my parents' living room, amid drawn curtains and a tense deferential hush. We had brought my father home from the hospital to die, but against all odds he appeared to be making a comeback: he could raise his head a little way, expectorate a few raspy words. Although he spent the greater part of his days dozing, his hearing was like a bat's sonar. You'd try creeping past the living room to get to the kitchen, or—for the blessed relief of it—to leave the house for a short while, and he'd call out or start moaning. I or my mother or my sister (we were functionally interchangeable) would quietly pad over to the bed and whisper encouragements, attempting to soothe him as one might soothe a small child.

"So short!" He said it a few times, referring to his life, the unfathomable brevity of it and the horrible realization that there was nothing to be done. It hardly mattered that he had enjoyed eighty-seven long years of the vital stuff. Or that the vast majority of those years had, by any common measure, been easy. All he could focus on was the end and his crushing desire to avert it.

I was at my father's side much of the time in those final weeks, a witness to both the gifts and miseries of being near death. Nurses came and went, patient, long-suffering. They sat beside him for hours at a time, dousing spongy lollipops in water and then rolling the wet and heavy heads over his parched lips so he might receive a scant few drops. They held his hand when he raved, the victim of morphine-induced hallucinations, and changed the dressings on his ulcerated legs. Oh, those legs. They were truly painful to behold: matchstick thin, purple, the skin cracked—and no good for walking, though he didn't always understand that. Once, he beckoned me over in a state of alarm, signaling with a bony finger for me to lean in. I put my ear to his mouth. "Someone's broken my legs," he said, the urgent words slipping and gurgling over the water in his lungs. "Help me."

There's a famous line from a Basil Bunting poem that says, "It is easier to die than to remember." No matter the care and precision with which the stonemason in Bunting's poem wields his mallet and chisel, his marks are destined for erasure: "Name and date / split in soft slate / a few months obliterate."

The lines came to me in those awful weeks when I realized just how bloody hard it is to die. The body will not be easily stilled; its pumps and circuits and muscles and pulleys resist shutdown. How a body as incapacitated as my father's managed to fight back with such punch astounded me. It is a lesson I will not soon forget.

Remembering, by contrast, was like a subterranean lake of crude that had just been struck by a Texan drill: it spurted out forcefully, unstoppable, and at all hours, day or night. My father's childhood, in particular, came back to him in vivid scenes, like a streaming video projected across the drawn curtains at the far end of the room. Across the velvety folds he saw himself, a boy in shorts, at the family house—vast, lime-washed—in colonial Rangoon, skating over polished hardwood floors in his stockinged feet. A miniature Fred Astaire. Or he watched himself tour the garden's grassy groves, loitering, idling, waiting for curious insects on leaves to take flight, or for swans to push off from the end of the huge pond that his Iraqi Jewish father had built at the bottom of his wannabe-English lawn.

At night my father remembered the dead. They came to him in his dreams, pleading; his mother wrapped in her shawl, wringing her hands, his grandparents smiling and nodding. He must come, they said. He must join them. Bathed in the hazy glow of fond remembrance—warm, inviting—they'd entreat him, and my father would be seductively drawn in. He'd feel his spirit keening, his heart longing, his whole being forgetful of where it belonged, wanting to respond, only for him to awaken suddenly, shaken by an eleventh-hour horror of what actually heeding those ghostly callings might mean.

It puzzled me then and it puzzles me now, but right until the end he did not want to go. Bedridden, acutely dehydrated, barely able to move except for a bothersome agitation in his hands, pumped with sedatives, his breathing aided by oxygen, his bowels emptied into disposable paper pants, he clung determinedly on. Much of the time he was delirious, and he could not sleep for feverish dreams. He vomited in reaction to his meds and railed against the unfairness of it all. But still he would not countenance a final departure.

At first I put this inability to let go down to his having unfinished business to attend to (he wanted to see loved ones one last time, and to set his mind at ease about my mother's welfare). I assumed, wrongly, that he entertained ideas about a "good death." To my mind, the tableau before me resembled a medieval painting in which the viewer was meant to read a parable of just that: an old man reclining on his deathbed, his body wasted, yet lavishly robed, and a long file of well-wishers in attendance, come to say their respectful good-byes.

I remember thinking at the time that my father was never more dignified than when he lay dying. Reanimated by the attentions of loved ones, he managed to prize open a tiny chink in the gloaming through which the last of the sun's rays might shine: he would blow a kiss at a grandchild or squeeze the hand of a relative in confidence. Occasionally he succeeded in smiling a crooked smile, defying the slack-jawed myopathy that afflicts the dying, when the mouth forms itself into the dreaded Q-shape that doctors know as a sign of approaching death.

We, the women of the family, in a family of women, fluttered about, bringing before him grandchildren, brothers, equally aged school friends, sons-in-law, cousins; like magicians pulling rabbits out of hats, we were eager to please. We stroked his hair and stilled his fretful hands, and we reminded him of good times. When he thanked me for these stringlike runs of small ministrations—"You are a lovely person," he said—tears sprang from my eyes like water jets. It was the first time in my life he had ever expressed such gratitude.

His unfinished business done, however, my father panicked. There was nothing left he could think of to do—and nothing to divert him from the knowledge of how little he actually could do. Only later would I allow the suspicion to form that my father's terror of dying had its origins elsewhere, and that the *ars moriendi* was of no metaphysical concern to him. For though an octogenarian on the outside, inside he was still a child.

Once this notion took hold, it stuck. I knew its rightness in my bones. In spite of appearances, my father had never grown up. He was the *puer aeternus*, the eternal boy, who, in the scheme of emotional development outlined by Carl Jung, forever identified with the pristine, omnipotent, infinitely possible self that characterizes the childhood ego. That self had remained intact through any number of disappointments, bereavements, and geographical relocations, not to mention marriage, fatherhood, and the unarguable signs of aging. At eighty-seven, my father was still a boy in shorts, skipping around the garden. He was monarchic, demanding and filled with utterly impractical heroic intentions:

"I am thinking of going to the south of France for a few days, just to see the sun," he announced one day; he was eighty-four at the time and shortly to become the dependent owner of a walking frame.

To all intents and purposes my father's long life resembled a closed loop: he went only so far along life's road and then, developmentally speaking, he retraced the path back to source. Put another way, he spent the second half of his life future-proofing himself, squandering its opportunities for reflection and learning, and with that its opportunities for novelty, joy, and surprise.

At one level, I sympathize with his rage against time's maddening shortness. A middle-aged woman, I've begun to experience the accelerating years myself: there is the evidence in the mirror, startling and nonnegotiable. But I've become acquainted with an everyday acceleration as well, the way successive nights and weeks and months seem to tailgate one another with increasing insistence, like the turning pages of a book of animation: flip, flip, flip, flip, flip, flip. And there I am, a line figure kicked from page to page, tripping up over myself, barely able to take stock of my surroundings before being kicked on toward the final scene, and my own all-too-human conclusion.

My father's furious backpedaling, I now see, was the best he could do with limited tools. Then again, if time's trickery is a matter of degree, with increasing age winding up the torque, then perhaps by the time you get to eighty-seven you can only wonder at how entire decades are crunched down, or forcibly compacted, the way bodies of cars are reduced to dense cubes of metal with no beginning or end; or with beginning and end welded together into a state that defies any narrative extension.

* * *

As soon as my father was gone, my reality was kinked. I was father-less. I felt dizzied by the number of implications and consequences that tumbled from this new state and which I knew would take many months to absorb, let alone process. This, at least, was what I thought. What I *did* was take myself to the gym.

Every morning I sprang from my insomnia-soiled bed, the sheets rucked and reeking with anxiety, and walked the five minutes from my house to the pump house across the frigid winter tarmac and over a litter-strewn canal, where bits of plastic, white as jellyfish, bobbed alongside discarded bicycles whose twisted frames mirrored my mangled insides. Frequently I got there before the guy with the keys who opened the doors at 6:30 a.m. We'd exchange pleasantries (how was it possible that I could still do such a thing?) and then I made straight for the treadmill. I plugged myself into the sound box, pounding my feet to the rhythm of whatever beat was on offer, seeing my heart rate climb to 140, then 160, and watched dawn break over the Regent's Canal, my mind as blissfully blank as the TV screens on the wall opposite.

I liked the inhumanity of the fitness arena, its hard angles and rubbery smell, the factory roar of the industrial fans. Its insensibility to my sorrow was pure balm. Most days I ran like someone possessed—past pain and past tiredness, in a fever to rid myself of surplus energy. I had energy for three. I had horsepower. I thought that if you hooked me up to a generator, I could make coffee grinders grind and lightbulbs shine.

In the gym I pursued strength. I wanted to become a machine myself, as if by making pistons of my muscles and injection valves of my arteries I might place myself beyond mortality. I hankered after the ropy arms that women's magazines write about with disgust, dreamed of seeing my veins bulge and pop. I wanted to make myself into a mechanized thing that articulated itself through the language of resistance. It never occurred to me that in my mania for self-maintenance (for wanting to remain the same) I'd plumped for exactly the course of action my father had taken in his war against time.

Of course, it is in the gym more than anywhere else that you know you've lost the fight to remain young, that your body is no longer a temple, but a jalopy. A few months into my obsessive workout regime I developed tendinitis and was banned from running for six months. Then my scoliosis began to play up in protest against all that pounding and made a mockery of my attempts to sleep. This was the aging body manifesting itself, as if in relief, against my father's death. Faulty, broken, it was telling me that I needed to look elsewhere for survival techniques. That aging and mourning deserved a classier kind of attention.

Wanting to get to grips with the buried reasons behind my antics, I turned to Jung, remembering from university days that the Swiss psychoanalyst had underscored how important it was, for healing, to integrate the unconscious mind into the knowing self. Unlike Freud, for whom the unconscious was a Pandora's box of repressed sexual drives, Jung believed the unconscious was a richer place, populated by ancient and mythic archetypes that had been transmitted, memelike, down the generations. It was a venerable repository of collective human wisdom. Returning to Jung now, I discovered that he was also a keen diagnostician of midlife.

In 1930, when he was himself fifty-five, Jung wrote a paper titled "The Stages of Life," in which he put forward a loose first-half/second-half model of life's progress, likening it to the rising and setting of the sun over the course of a very long day. As the sun ascends, said Jung (emerging, like a babe from the womb, from a "nocturnal sea of unconsciousness"), it looks upon the bright world and its field of action, gradually rising to its zenith. At this point of maximum brightness, individuals attain full adult identity: they will have achieved mature relationships and a solid career, found stability in their personal lives and confidence in their dealings with the world. Of course, this "culminating point cannot be calculated or known in advance, only when it starts to move beyond it, when you are aware of descending."

Then, once the descent has begun, you get "the reversal of all the ideals and values that were cherished in the morning." This is as it should be, said Jung. Because if we try to live the second half of our lives as we lived the first, we will fail in the task of self-realization. The sun, to use his words, must fall into "a contradiction with itself . . . as though it should draw its rays in instead of emitting them." This inward-looking movement, or reflective self-examination—when the sun's rays illuminate itself, a process Jung saw as innately spiritual—leads us to reject the false gods of our youth and embark on a journey that has as its goal the reconciliation of the ego to the true self, shadow side and all.

In this bell-shaped picture of rise and fall, midlife is the apex that cannot be seen. Only it doesn't feel like an apex, because what happens to the psyche at this stage is fundamentally destabilizing. What happens is this: The persona, which is the public, surface self that our egos project to the world, starts to crack. It cannot be sustained. What's more, at some level we recognize that it cannot be sustained. Our impulse (quite natural) is to paper over the cracks, to prop up the persona and continue to project its smiling face to the world, even though we no longer believe in its integrity.

This, I saw at once, is what I was doing in the gym. I was propping up my false self, thinking, largely unconsciously, that if I worked hard enough at the job of physical maintenance, then nothing need change; as in, I need not move forward to meet my end, like my father. With the hedge that stood between me and my mortality removed, I was "acting out" a new awareness of death.

Through Jung, I was beginning to understand that to regain a healthy psyche one needed to dismantle the persona (or bury the corpse of our false self) by recognizing that the naggings of our egos—heroic, ambitious, unattainable—will never be met. This can feel like a critical defeat, but it also allows us to free the ego to explore different forms, and to liberate our shadow selves from the dungeons of repression.

This is when, for example, the man who in his primary relationships always tried to mother his partner realizes that he has been engaged in a futile attempt to be the mother he never had. Finally he admits the difficult truth that she was never there for him. Or when the woman who has spent decades acting out her parents' projections of success recognizes the fantasies that she mistook for real and learns that it is okay, even necessary, to fail. It's the sort of midlife jump my father was unable to make. I didn't want to fail, as he did, at this critical hurdle, condemning myself to "live the afternoon of life according to the programme of life's morning." I didn't want to be, as he was, estranged from the future—which condition ultimately rendered him incapable of preparing for his death. And so the part of Jung I consumed most hungrily was where he talks about his own midlife trauma.

Jung was famously reluctant to air his personal life in public, but in his early eighties he allowed himself to be coaxed into cowriting (with Swiss analyst Aniela Jaffé) an intellectual autobiography, posthumously published in 1963 as *Memories, Dreams, Reflections,* in which he was astonishingly candid about his childhood, his religious experiences, his break with Freud, his periods of desperate self-doubt.

It is in this book that Jung described his own midlife transition as a period in which he entered a kind of intellectual wilderness. He found himself incapable of reading a scientific book and unable to talk about what really preoccupied him. He decided to abandon his academic career, just like that ("What, after all, did it matter whether or not I became a professor?"), and he plunged himself deep into uncertainty. Jung describes the period as a time of "extreme loneliness" and searching. Obsessively, he drew and painted mandalas, brightly colored, enigmatic, self-embroidering, convinced that the circular imagery contained a message about the meaning of life—and equally convinced that only by solving that puzzle would he emerge from the darkness that had enveloped him after he broke with Freud, then academia itself. He says that while he intuited his life's mission at this point, which was to fully articulate how the goal of psychic development was the self (that is, an integrated picture—like a mandala—of the persona, ego, shadow, and animus or anima), it took him another twenty years to really understand the effusions of his own unconscious that erupted at this midlife point, fiery and effulgent as a stream of lava.

More than anything else, it was the darkness that Jung described navigating at this time that spoke to me, since this was something I now felt myself submerged in. I was besieged by black thoughts. I had attributed this journey into darkness to my grief over the triple loss I'd endured—of youth, reproductive life, a parent—over a period short enough for it to feel like a single developmental moment. But while the feeling was grieflike, the outward manifestation was paralysis.

Most agonizing to me was that I was incapable of writing a word. For a year and more I was completely mute, struck dumb not just by the hammering events whose aftershocks I had no idea how to manage, but also by the sense that all around me was fog and murk. If I couldn't see anything clearly, then how could I write about it? Or, indeed, write at all.

Perhaps my biggest mistake at this time was to try to write about my father. I had embarked on a fashion memoir, pegged loosely to his life in couture, before he became desperately ill, when I abandoned it. But then, when he died and everything was raw and indigestible, I foolishly picked it up again in the mad hope that it would give me back what I could not have, that writing him up was as good as a resurrection.

The unconscious mind is a marvelous thing, and mine tried to solve my paralysis for me. I applied for a half-time job as an editor so that I could remain close to words, coaxing them out of others when I could not draw them from myself. But the words I processed daily washed over me like water moving over rocks in a stream. I already felt as if every ounce of creative juice in me had been drained; now I saw that if there were any ideas left in me, they, too, would leach out and trickle away. There was little point in fighting it, this accidie. I simply had to stay the course and pray that when the time was right the urge to pick up a pen would spring back to form like a muscle memory.

There is a term for this gnomic state I found myself in, beloved of anthropologists who study the significance of ritual and the purpose of rites of passage. That term is *liminal*, from the Latin *limen*, meaning "threshold," though it has much in common with *limbus*, meaning "marginal"—the root from which we get *limbic* (as in the primitive brain) and also the sense of inertia we call limbo.

In moving through a liminal phase the mind untethers itself from what it knows in order to drift and float toward new modes of being. The mind is in transit. Freed from the strictures and patterns of temporality, specifically the straitjacket of cause and effect, it moves associatively through wanderings and the play of dreams, and via insights and aperçus. In byways and slipstreams it revels in its own backtrackings and circumambulations, and, in so doing, remakes itself by stealth.

Liminality describes how you perceive things and intuit connections when you are in the midst of casting aside old habits, convictions, and ways of being in the world, but are still desperately unsure of what you are groping toward. I had been in this place before—when I returned to the world's busy thoroughfares after my hysterectomy and clearly felt myself to exist both inside time and out of it. Now I was here again. Unconsciously I was on the move. And so, consciously, I decided to embrace movement.

As the year in which I was turning fifty dawned, I decided I needed to shake things up. Mine is a summer birthday, and so I had six months to set the wheels of change in motion. I knew that I wanted more control over my time. I also wanted to push myself back into writing by removing the layers of financial stability that I had acquired, like padding, to shore myself up when I was at my most fragile. But now I felt emboldened: if my persona was being dismantled come what may, I told myself, then I would welcome instability.

Then a strange thing happened. I discovered that I missed my father—and with a longing that threw me for a loop, for until his final illness our relationship had been a ruin. Shot through with bullet holes from years of constant sniping was a whole history together that was irreparably scarred.

My father may have been clueless about how to die, but he had in many ways mastered the art of how to live. Though never wealthy (and when he was ahead, he blew his money on gambling—or travel, or diamond necklaces my mother never once coveted), he somehow convinced himself, and plenty of other people, too, that he was born to live a life of luxury. He disdained the ordinary in all things—cheap clothing, bad food, commonplace addictions such as alcohol or tobacco, though of course he had his own Achilles' heel on that score—and he pursued finery in all its forms. He showered trinkets and furs on my unshowy mother and bought himself the best suits (and shirts and socks and underwear). He never skimped on a good meal either: "Whatever it costs, it costs!" He practiced a kind of arm-sweeping monetary bravado, profligate and impulsive. Only my mother's cleverness with cash kept them afloat.

Most of the time my father inhabited a bubble world of his own making. He lovingly embroidered his exotic childhood in Burma and Palestine, and bigged up his career as a couturier in Paris, working for the House of Dior. So much puff was in play, such an excess of alluring smoke and megaphoned achievement, designed to impress, that it was impossible to tell what was real from what was not. Not that this bothered him: he saw reality as an inconvenience, something to get beyond, or to squash like a troublesome gnat.

As I was one of the beneficiaries of his largesse (generosity being another lavish quality he cultivated, since he liked to live big), my childhood was an exultation of long-haul travel—across Africa, India, Australia—and fine dining. It was a world-widening experience, unusual for the era I grew up in, and I am eternally grateful for having been given it. The home front was just as exciting. Every so often my father would hit on a new restaurant, then take us there each weekend until he tired of the place. There was a rustic French bistro in Belsize Park that we went to for a couple of years; and a hotel near Heathrow Airport where you could sip coconut mocktails with mini-umbrellas in an indoor garden planted with palms, its tropical aspirations completed by a heated pool and steel band. The hotel appealed to my father's taste for kitsch: if he couldn't have the real thing, he'd much rather take a camp substitute over a poor man's holiday.

If there were friends he could invite along on these assorted excursions, so much the better, since that way he'd have a worthy audience for his stories. And he was a raconteur of world-class ability. He could have been spouting rubbish, and he often did, but he could hold people spellbound with his anecdotes from Burma, or postwar Paris, or the celebrity-strewn fashion world into which he had dipped a professional toe, though he would claim that he bestrode it like a colossus.

My father had always wanted daughters. He wanted daughters to mold and groom and marry off. And daughters he got. But nervy, brainy ones who wished to go their own way, and with puritanical streaks that chafed against his voluptuary nature. And so we clashed and clashed again. In the end I carved out a path for myself so different from the one he had rosily envisioned that beyond the tug of family loyalty I barely felt connected to him.

But then there arises the problem of generational succession— that fragile chain of vertical connection that is most noticeable when it breaks. The breakage can be symbolic, when, for example, and as any midlifer knows who has experienced firsthand how the tables can turn, the parents become the children and the child the parent. Or it can be as literal (and as ordinary) as a parent dying. Either way, it calls for some deft rearranging of one's mental furniture, an accommodation of some new and ugly heirloom piece that you have to get used to, and normalize.

It is a truism that when a parent dies you're suddenly confronted with your mortality: whereas before there had always been a fall guy to take the hit for you, now you have to negotiate your own end. But I have come to believe that with this awareness of succession one also begins to scratch around for loose threads that might be tied back into the previous generation, and that go some way toward repairing a sense of loss. Think of it as a kind of emotional darning.

One such tie between my father and me was that we agreed, unequivocally, on the nonexistence of an afterlife. You had your time and then you turned to dust. It was a reflex thing for my father. He wasn't convinced by the afterlife: end of story. No philosophical agonizing was involved. Looking back, I think his imprisonment in the magical thinking of childhood served him well on this score. It meant he didn't just deny death, he refused it: if there was nowhere it led to, he wasn't going to have it.

For my part, I've always been especially unconvinced by the idea of a bodily resurrection (and the taxidermist deity that goes with it). On the other hand, if there *is* an afterlife, it seems risible to me that it should take the shape of an Edenic throwback, flowing with milk and honey and wine: an eternal day spent lazing, or cavorting in music and song. If I try to imagine a realistic afterlife, the best I can do is imagine a free-floating consciousness that continues ad nauseam to fret over whether the terrestrial life ("So short!") had been well spent after all. Which translates, more or less, into an eternity on the analyst's couch.

It makes sense to me, as it made sense to my father, that life is a finite thing. I'm not saying that I share his refusenik stance toward dying, but I do understand why he was unable to make peace with its inevitability. And it does rather put the onus back on how well you manage to live. Perhaps he got that right after all.

So what else do I miss?

I miss his naked and unashamed appetite for living.

I miss his appreciation of beautiful things.

I miss his warmth.

I miss his way of scrunching up both eyes because he could never master the conspiratorial wink.

I miss his sense of adventure, large and small.

I miss the slightly reckless feeling of riskiness that hung about him like a cologne—part sweat, part excitement, part dare.

I miss his laughter.

God help me, I even miss his stories.

There was the time, for instance, when the Hollywood actress Cyd Charisse invited him to her room at the Dorchester Hotel to measure those legendary legs for a dress, but then she wouldn't stand still long enough for him to pin it. "Miss Charisse," my father said, a little sternly (and here he'd pause for effect), "I leg you to just keep still." Was it true? I'll never know and I don't really care.

Then there was the maid who cleaned his student lodgings in Paris, and who told him that she'd pushed a German soldier under a train during the war. She had sat on my father's bed, desolate and tearful, her hair falling out of its bun, her fingers worrying at the loose strands. She was in distress not because she was consumed with guilt, but because she'd only managed to fell one of the bastards.

Then there was the time his then roommate, the son of a Greek diplomat, and as pampered a student as my father, tried to get him to eat rabbit. A meat eater to his core, but enslaved by the laws of kashruth, my father had recoiled from the challenge by pretending he was vegetarian. Of course the next night at the pension they shared there was chicken—his favorite thing in the world—but fixed from across the dining room by his roommate's eagle eye, he had to suffer an omelet instead.

English was my father's fourth language, and he was prone to slips when using it. One evening, not long before his final illness, after we had dined well and the family had repaired to the living room, he began on an ordinary story about his travels. He was in Malta, where he'd felt obliged to wine and dine a client. But then he'd mischievously ducked out of the evening to seek out the preferable company of the hotel room's TV. "But every channel I found, it was all the same," he complained: "All prawn. There was prawn everywhere."

First there was a titter, then a giggle, then a chuckle, before the entire room exploded in uncontrollable laughter, each of us unable to get out of his or her head the curious image of an orgy of squirming crustaceans—antennae waving, tiny legs kicking. We laughed until we cried and coughed and spluttered. And then we laughed some more.

My father, at first, was thrilled to have generated such jollity. But then the penny dropped: we were not laughing with him. Momentarily his face froze.

I saw a fleeting shadow pass across his visage, transfiguring his features for a fraction of a beat. I thought I saw pique. I definitely saw confusion. And there was a tiny waver of confidence, too. But no sooner had these impressions formed than they dissolved, giving way to a what-the-hell expression, and he let us laugh ourselves out. In the end he was able to rejoice in having created such hilarity, even if he happened to be its subject.

He had handled the fudging with aplomb. I'm not sure that I would have.

If he were still alive, my prawn-star dad, I wonder what he would make of his daughter hitting the half-century mark. Although I think I know. I think that a man as eternally boyish as he would simply declare it impossible.

Perhaps it is just as well that I will turn fifty in his absence. My father would not have understood or, if he had, sympathized with my systematic disassembly of the persona I had clung to for much of my adult life. He would have been afraid of the psychic unmooring demanded by liminality, by the rite of passage that insists you strip yourself down before the threshold of midlife. So, on balance, when it comes to fretting about generational succession, I am glad that it is my daughter who is now firmly in my sights.

Heart

EVERY FEW WEEKS MY DAUGHTER AND I STAND BACK-TO-BACK IN the kitchen, socks off, our bare feet cooling on the tiled floor, and we measure up. I feel her body elongate itself at my back, straining upward, squaring preteen shoulders against my sloping ones, while our bottoms, cushioned one against the other, are taut with tension. We look like a totem pole—bodies melded together, stony faces pointing outward, chins up, and arms pressed against our sides. My husband circles us, bending his knees to get all the angles and squinting like a surveyor. "Not quite there yet," he says. "There's about two inches in it." Later he confesses to being spooked. "Looking at the two of you is like witnessing time travel," he tells me.

My daughter, who initiated this household ritual, has already dispensed with one yardstick: just before she turned twelve, she overtook my mother. In her stride now, she is visibly delighted to be gaining on me. Standing on tiptoe and flinging an arm around my shoulder, she tries out equality and likes it. Soon enough there'll be no need for any artificial elevation. We will be peers, in the matter of height if nothing else.

My husband has already lost his way with the laundry. My daughter's knickers, candy striped and tartan checked, regularly turn up in my drawers, while my tights have begun disappearing into hers. She appropriates them, naturally, and wears them in the new style: opaque legs in black or navy under cutoff denim shorts. All the girls dress this way, come rain or shine, their toenails poking holes into their mothers' tights.

I've begun to see his category errors as a way of redrawing the boundaries of our parenting duties. Having shared the job with me in a genuinely egalitarian, straight-down-the-middle fashion for the first twelve years of our daughter's life, he now, however unconsciously, seems to feel that our concerns fork into he-matters and she-matters. Underwear has become my domain, in consequence of which he need not task himself in thinking too hard about it. My own need to recalibrate my relationship to our daughter is just as pressing. But it is of a different order. Every mother meets the paradox that the more her daughter is drawn into womanhood, the more she pulls away. It is a confusing social induction that appears to obey strange magnetic rules: daughters are attracted to the adult world of women, but repelled by their actual mothers. Their resistance is primal, and fundamentally self-protective: for how is a girl to acquire a distinct sense of her identity when every pubescent change her body undergoes threatens to blend her into a confusing mélange with the woman who birthed her?

It is little wonder the father-daughter bond is often so strong—which is another thing mothers must contend with. In my household, watching *Star Trek* reruns and end-to-end episodes of *The Simpsons* are both folies à deux, as are American pancake feasts, not caring that the dog stinks, loafing in baggy T-shirts, confecting newfangled desserts late at night, ice-skating, planning camping trips that never happen, and more. I'd be lying if I said I didn't mind being excluded, even if this all sets a reassuringly high bar for the men who may come into my daughter's life later. But I take her affinity for difference to be largely unavoidable. If a daughter is to properly separate from her mother, then it stands to reason that she will cement that opposition by forging closer ties with her father.

Where this developmental dynamic is confined to just three souls, it is all the more potent. What complicates matters further is my own need to detach from her. This is a developmental issue, particularly poignant for women in midlife, and seldom given proper attention.

If my daughter and I tussle it is because *each of us*, not just her, is striving to find her own ground: I, to sever myself from the young woman I once was, and of whom she so strongly reminds me; she, from a tyrannous feeling that she's a mini-me—not just a doppelgänger, but her mother-in-training.

At the cusp of adolescence, she is changing in ways that feel peculiar and unexpected—flesh filling out nascent curves, thick hairs sprouting willfully. With her biorhythms synced to a wayward chemistry, she's become moody, lippy, and incredibly self-conscious (privacy is now permanently manifested with a capital *P*). A smart girl, she's grasped that the source of her discomfort is the oddity of standing with one foot in childhood and the other in proto-adulthood. Her instinct is to hold firm to the ground she knows. While her classmates experiment with makeup and teenage posturing, she seems reluctant to put away childish things. It is as if she's intuited that these next months will be her last hurrah when it comes to Minecraft, Calico Critters, secret spy books, and a lingering affection for the scantily clad superpower fairies of the cartoon franchise *Winx Club*.

I've never felt us to be more mirrored. In middle age, my body is also changing in surprising ways: my skin is crepey, my joints click and pop. While her hormones rage, mine are plummeting. She's discovered sleep; I'm suddenly insomniac. Her memory is a fine-tuned thing; mine is perpetually tripping up. At the same time, both of us ricochet between crankiness and euphoria. As if this were not upheaval enough, to my great irritation I am once again prone to glaring outbursts of acne, just as she breaks out in spots. After decades of feeling comfortable in my skin I, too, am now deeply self-conscious.

Not surprisingly, ours is a household of fireworks; one of us, my daughter or me, can always be relied upon to ignite the other's latent combustibility.

But what is really at the root of our twinship? Is it simply a product of my having postponed having children until my late thirties, so that my daughter hits adolescence just as I encounter menopause? Is it really just a numbers game? Or is there more to my identifying with her every bit as much as she identifies with me? The last thing I need, after all, is to yield to that backward pull and slide from the solid ground of the present into the runnels my father was so comfortable inhabiting, regularly flooded by the runoff of memory and awash with the fragrant past.

Suzanne Braun Levine, the original editor of *Ms.* magazine, who has lately reinvented herself as a guru of the midlife crisis, invokes the phrase "Second Adulthood" to describe a phase of "existential bewilderment" that afflicts women in midlife and is every bit as traumatic as adolescence. As we enter it, we wobble. We question everything we once took for granted. We experiment, reevaluate, take risks, confront our fears, ask ourselves who we are and where we think we're going. Our metaphysical, practical, and emotional concerns collapse together as they are brought to bear on a single question: our suddenly malleable identity. This evaluative project suggests that there is more to mother-daughter mirroring than either biology or chronology can account for. But Levine is merely a popularizer: the key to that *more* is to be found in the work of the German-born developmental psychologist Erik Erikson.

Erikson, who died in 1994, at the age of ninety-one, coined the term *identity crisis*. A devoted follower of Freud's, as a young man he moved to Vienna and threw himself into a crucible of psychoanalytic ferment, training with the Gestalt psychologists Karl and Charlotte Bühler, and eventually with Anna Freud. Later, he would liken those years to "the Paulinian days of Christianity." The analogy is telling, since Freud's early apostles would also rewrite the basic creed for a new generation of acolytes. With Hitler's rise to power, Erikson left Europe for America, where he held a succession of posts in prestigious universities as a specialist in the field of child psychoanalysis.

Over the coming decades, Erikson (like Jung before him) would deviate from Freudian orthodoxy in a number of highly significant ways. He came to believe, for example, that the ego was more than merely a servant of the id (implying that we are less subject to inner drives and more influenced by our conscious desires), and that the wider environment in which a child lived was as critical to her emotional development and identity formation as the psychodynamics of her family. He also came to see development as a lifelong process—not as something that was formed and fixed in infancy, as Freud had always insisted. Just as parents influenced a child's development, argued Erikson, they were, in turn, profoundly affected by their children.

In 1950, and with a good deal of unsung input from his Canadian wife, Joan, Erikson came up with a seven-stage theory of personality development, inspired by Shakespeare's seven ages of man, that has since become a cornerstone of adult development theory. Each stage was characterized by a "psychosocial crisis," and this crisis had to be resolved before a person could progress to the next stage. If unresolved, the result was a kind of arrested development. One day, while driving Erik from their Berkeley home to the train station in South San Francisco, Joan had a revelation: "Hey, we left ourselves out," she shouted. They were both forty-eight. By the time they'd reached the station platform, the Eriksons had fleshed out an eight-stage development model, now including a phase they called generativity, which represented middle age.

Each Eriksonian stage brings with it a form of enrichment, or "virtue." Adulthood, for example (covering, roughly, the ages twenty to forty), sees the individual forging solid relationships and lifelong partnerships through negotiating a psychosocial crisis that pits the needs of intimacy against those of isolation. Its associated virtue is love. Whereas the succeeding midlife crisis (occurring in stage seven, late adulthood, roughly forty to sixty-five) demands that we embrace "generativity" over self-absorption and go on to embody the virtue of "care." If we fail to do this, we run the risk of stagnating and of sliding into unhappy narcissism.

By generativity, Erikson included all kinds of giving back to society: the production of art, the reproduction of children, the support offered to younger generations, a deeper engagement with society. As Erikson put it, "An adult must be ready to become a numinous model in the next generation's eyes and to act as a judge of evil and a transmitter of ideal values."

All of this rings true to me, especially the idea that there is no single self, only multiple selves, or a succession of selves; that we keep changing, keep growing. It suggests that real gains might be had from midlife's tribulations, not just weak consolations, and that life's arc might trace an upward curve instead of a slow downward spiral.

As an added boon to my mother-daughter mirroring, the generative agenda suggests that my daughter and I move forward in parallel, each of us unmooring from one stagnant self and chugging off along life's meandering stream to find another. Perhaps, in fact, it is only in consequence of this mutual separation that we will eventually find our way back to each other.

Erikson's eight-stage development model was extremely influential in America, though it remained unpopular with the psychoanalytic fraternity in Europe, to whom it seemed, well, rather too accommodating of life. In shifting the emphasis from psychosexual trauma to psychosocial crises, the model located the struggle to achieve a stable identity not in the permanent internal warfare of the psyche, as Freud had done, but in the tension between self and society. With studied application, argued Erikson, that tension might be resolved in the individual's favor, leading to psychic peace. This, if you like, was the goal of midlife development.

However, whether Erikson managed to resolve this tension in his own life is debatable. His biographer Lawrence J. Friedman believes that the Eriksons never came to enjoy psychic peace because they were keepers of a dreadful secret that undermined the picture-perfect family image they so assiduously maintained in public.

In 1944, Joan gave birth to her fourth child, Neil. But the happy event was marred by the news that Neil was born with Down syndrome, a condition that was then poorly understood. Down's children were not expected to live long, and if they did, they were deemed too "retarded" to survive in the social and educational mainstream. A decade or so later the American pediatrician Benjamin Spock would revolutionize such thinking, and with it the fortunes of Down's children, by recommending that their lives should be as normal as possible and that they should remain at home with their parents and siblings. But in the 1940s such children were routinely institutionalized.

With Joan under heavy sedation after Neil's birth, doctors at the hospital pressed Erik to agree to send Neil away before mother and baby formed a strong attachment bond. Erik was distraught. But after consulting his good friend the anthropologist Margaret Mead, he agreed to the dastardly pact. Neil would be sent away immediately, and no one need ever know that he had survived birth—including two of the Erikson's three existing children.

Friedman is convinced that Erikson's guilt over this decision led him to focus on mapping out a thoroughgoing scheme of normal development—one that might buoy the family of five who thrived at home in Berkeley, uncompromised by the taint of genetic aberration. He suggests, too, that the guilt of lying to their children by telling them that Neil had died was a driving force in the Eriksons' formulation of the generative stage of adult development. After all, had they not, as a couple, sacrificed care to the superego's demands of self-absorption?

Friedman's argument is tantalizing, especially when one considers the damage wrought when mother and child are prevented from attaching, and then from undergoing normal separation. I shudder to think of the developmental limbo that Joan Erikson was forced to endure as she entered middle age, assailed by doubts over the rightness of her and her husband's actions. In secret she visited Neil a number of times, but she found these visits increasingly upsetting and eventually she stopped going. Neil was withdrawn and unresponsive and thus unable to give Joan the dispensation she craved by rewarding her with some kind of relationship.

As a footnote to which, it is interesting that around the time Erik published *Childhood and Society* (1950), the book that would catapult him into the limelight, Joan arranged for the whole family to move to nearby Orinda, where she took up voluntary work at a local hospital helping patients with mental illness to reintegrate into the world.

In recent decades, the Eriksons' development model has been given an unexpected boost from research in neuroscience that has begun to uncover empirical evidence of significant developmental change in midlife. In the 1990s, Harvard Medical School research scientist Francine Benes made a pioneering discovery while studying adolescent brain development. Benes found that the adolescent brain undergoes a pronounced increase in myelination—myelination being a form of growth that boosts the brain's processing power by enhancing the way neurons conduct electrical signals. To highlight this peak in brain development, she and her colleagues compared the growth of the adolescent brain against a control group of 164 people, aged between zero and seventy-six. That's when Benes noticed a second spike: the brain, it transpired, underwent a second, and wholly unexpected, growth spurt in middle age. The implications for cognitive science were huge.

Harvard retains a pioneering role in this line of research. A 2013 edition of *On the Brain*, the newsletter of the university's Mahoney Neuroscience Institute, was devoted to a state-of-the-art survey of the middle-aged brain. Though still a young field, research into neuroplasticity—that is, the human brain's structural ability to reconfigure itself—is uncovering numerous ways in which designated specialist areas in the brain may be repurposed, rewired, or retrofitted and thus functionally transformed—although the extent to which life experience might spur such material change remains highly controversial.

Erik Erikson lived just long enough to learn about the rich findings in cognitive science that so resolutely back the development theory he formulated a half century earlier. I like to think that in reading about neuroplasticity he enjoyed cocking a final snook at Freud.

What I cherish about Erikson's model is the work it demands of us in progressing through its various stages. It pushes back against the self-help movement, with its lazy thinking and easy answers— and its chorus of witchy and wise female elders who treat middle age as some kind of wild electrical storm: something dark and brooding that gusts and howls, but dies down soon enough, most likely without blowing down too much collateral.

In the self-help model you are your "youniverse." By contrast, "generativity" suggests that midlife's rewards are the end products of hard work that displaces "you" from the center of your world. In other words, generativity is not something you can achieve in isolation. It is a process in which some kind of mirror is essential. Levine seems to grasp this, putting family dynamics into the mix when arguing that women empower themselves by channeling the mid-life storm. Viewed this way, development is relational, negotiated, a trade-off of one thing over another. But even Levine, at the sophisticated end of the self-help movement, does not want to acknowledge that before any kind of development, let alone rebirth, can occur, some mourning or grieving is essential. This mourning takes varied and complex forms, but among them is self-burial.

I am not generally sentimental, being of the firm opinion that sentiment blunts the intellect. But I am sentimental about my daughter: she is, as they say in the Arabic dialect of my Iraqi family, my *gulbi*—my heart.

When she was newborn, I felt an animal protectiveness over her future. I shed pay-it-forward tears for all the hurt she would inevitably experience over the course of her life. To my febrile postpartum brain, its entire course looked to be concertinaed into a series of worrying spikes: her first disappointment, her first bust up with a friend, her first heartbreak, her first loss—a whole world of pain that I had selfishly ushered her into. I put this maudlin cast of mind down to erratic hormones, but the sentimentality persisted.

Exhibit A: in my cupboard there is a shoebox in which I've stowed one representative of each of her early pairs of shoes, from the soft-soled, elasticized chamois she once toddled about in, to her first velcroed school shoes.

Exhibit B: in a tiny black-lacquered box with folding red-satin lining, I've kept the desiccated remains of the living cord that once bound us together. It was tied in a knot at her navel before she was handed to me, like a gift, at the birthing clinic, then it fell off, starved of blood supply, a couple of weeks later.

Exhibit C: another box—one I intend to return to her someday—of recreational work from her first ten years, contains choice drawings and painterly daubings, spy tales, mermaid diaries, notebooks filled with hilarious lists, and a card she made for my forty-eighth birthday, picturing a cake and candles, and captioned, "Mummy, we are all ageing!"

These days, I am practically infected with sentiment. But it has taken a new form—a nostalgia in which my own remembered (and now lost) youth has become entangled.

At its most insistent this nostalgia can floor me. I remember a particular afternoon in Paris, a few seasons back, during a short break with my husband and daughter. Basking in the spring sunshine and unseasonable April warmth, we had wandered through the staunchly bourgeois streets of Montparnasse, admiring the houses and fantasizing about inhabiting them, only to find that we had managed to wend our way to the Musée Rodin. Because of the conspiratorial magic we'd worked up among us, we felt as if it had somehow come to us, and that a visit was meant.

Inside the museum, an intimate space that had once been the sculptor's home, we split up, not deliberately, but each of us was absorbed in his or her own journey and intoxicated by different artworks that played on our different moods. Brilliant sunlight streamed into all the rooms, and the museum keepers had opened the tall windows, causing the light white voile curtains to dance on the breeze like triumphal banners. Upstairs, hardly a soul was around, and I ambled without aim from one room to the next, caught up in the joy of experiencing the tactile sculptures—the extraordinary rough sensuality captured in the head of Balzac, and the delicacy of expression in the gently arcing fingers belonging to a study of a pair of hands.

Suddenly I felt woozy. I can't tell exactly what the trigger was, a particular piece or room or mood, or simply the sultry feeling of being in a stifling space amid so much beautiful art—the syndrome named for Stendhal. But in that moment I was forcefully thrown back to an earlier visit, almost thirty years before, when I had toured this very museum with my then French lover. As if I'd been sucked bodily into a time tunnel, I was overcome by a vertiginous feeling of powerful desire—visceral, heady, deeply sexual, as if channeling all the hope and possibility my younger self had invested in that one soaring relationship. I felt practically faint with the memory of it, then, as I slowly returned to myself, desolate with a sense of loss.

Later, I tried explaining some of this to my husband, but as I struggled to convey what I meant (no, I was not consumed with longing for this lost lover, more a longing for my younger self, with autocrotic overtones), I realized that this was one of those experiences that ought not to be related. It lives in the felt moment and dies in the telling.

But the experience has stayed with me. And it has fine-tuned into a fierce ambivalence my feelings toward my daughter, as also my feelings about being her mother. I have never been more aware than I was at that moment of how an individual's different selves can telescope into one another, like collapsing lenses onto a single focal point, and effect a kind of time travel. You are at once here, and also there, or you are in several locations simultaneously. It creates an overwhelming sense of there being no concrete past, only a heavily accreted present, barnacled with the buildup of years gone by.

At the opposite end of the reproductive spectrum I am acutely aware of the threshold at which my daughter stands today. I want to wave at her in sympathy and recognition and assure her it will turn out well. I want to tell her that on the other side of this difficult adolescent transition there will be freedoms and experiences she's never dreamed of, as well as new heights of confidence and competence. There will be deep friendships and deeper loves, the roller coaster of university life and first jobs, independent travel, opportunities at every turn. I want to tell her that her dreams will become tangible. That her fears will drift into obscurity. That she will feel invincible.

But then I am overcome by a terrible sadness for my own lost opportunities, and by an ersatz nostalgia for paths not taken—a missing, if you like, of what I never had, and a misplaced anxiety about all the future paths I shall never take because with middle age comes a shrinking sense of the possible. Since half of me is lost in undifferentiated yearning for what might have been (and never will be), I am often unable to reassure my daughter with the right level of conviction. If I am to succeed in this task, I must first let go of my ghostly younger selves, not least the ones who can floor me, which is the grown-up version of putting away childish things.

What I can tell my daughter is that the world of unknowns before her is not so frightening as she thinks. Or, more accurately, it is less frightening than it is limiting—every choice freighted with the responsibility of eclipsing another choice: every road chosen, a path not taken.

Modern physics has come up with a comforting metaphor that addresses this anxiety about not being able to have it all: the many-worlds hypothesis. Originally developed by the American physicist Hugh Everett in 1957 as a response to the uncertainty inherent in quantum theory, the hypothesis has gone on to have a wider life as a thought experiment. According to the many-worlds idea, all possible histories and futures are real, because each time a decision has to be made the universe splits in two, ensuring that all outcomes are entertained. Every path you can imagine taking is actually taken, in one universe among a multitude of universes. Yet physics—however philosophically you slant it—is morally neutral: it cannot tell us in which universe our choices lead to greater fulfillment.

The many-worlds idea suggests to me that we ought to tear up our conventional blueprints. There is a road map for much of our lives, neatly plotted out. In simplistic guise it goes something like this: your teens are for studying, your twenties for experiments and fun; in your thirties you consolidate (careers, relationships, finances) and start parenting; then in your forties you acquire stature and kind of peak; and in your fifties, the horizon I am now looking toward, the lucky few get to peak again, while others experience middle age as a kind of mugging, robbing them of a feeling that the future might actually hold more than the past.

The theory suggests that this conventional, and admittedly first-world, blueprint is no better than any other prescribed path. In fact, it strikes me that those who hew most closely to its contours in youth end up feeling most lost in middle age. Where that leaves me in terms of counseling my daughter through adolescence is not entirely clear. But I wish to encourage her to embrace the Unknown. After all, with every step you take into the murk, the fog recedes a little.

In the best of my idealized scenarios, she and I journey into the unknown together as our mirroring continues. She departs from the blueprint as much as she likes, learning and adventuring by turn, while I venture into my foggy fifties, one air-clearing month at a time. There will be hard developmental work to do, and as much forgetting as generative reinventing. But all the while I can comfort myself that in other universes, far, far away, a series of other fifty-year-old me's will be suffering every fate that I've managed to escape: early retirement, divorce, grumpiness and general depression, loss of hope, lassitude, and bankruptcy.

Guts

THERE IS A STORY I WOULD LIKE TO TELL MY MOTHER AND SO begin a conversation about aging, hers and mine, and the different ways we manage it. This is not a subject we tend to discuss in the usual way, since our communications are governed by a comforting pattern of to-and-fro, rhythmic and accommodating, creating a warp and weft of empathy that works against rational understanding. That, or we explode at each other. In our everyday exchanges, my mother and I arrive at mutuality by omission. We bond around the edges of this and that.

Today our relationship is overshadowed by paperwork. By the power of attorney she wishes to hand me, so that I might manage her health care and finances in the event of her becoming doolally, and by the endless stream of stuff she needs to sign that pours through the letterbox, and which my mother, formerly a power-house of organizational efficiency, now wishes to have nothing to do with. When I visit, I am invited on a tour of cupboards in which she's stowed documents relating to the house or her savings, her will or share portfolio, the expectation being that I will somehow remember what is where so that she can forget about it. My mother believes in dispersal, as if storing everything in one place would imperil the integrity of her papered fortress.

Up a ladder one day, my head stuck in the musty innards of the spare-room cupboard, looking for some bit of officialdom my mother wishes to retrieve, I stumble across a scraggy plastic bag, all knotted up. Coiled inside it, like so many snakes, is her most precious jewelry, cold and clinking. All those diamonds my father went out on a financial limb to buy for her, wrapped up willy-nilly and tossed into the hold. "Where would I wear them now?" says my mother. Looking down at her standing at the bottom of the ladder in her sensible shoes and the comfort clothing she prefers, eyes angled over the tops of her varifocals, I can't think of a way to counter her. But my find gives me pause: Did my mother plant the bag there for me to stumble upon, the better to understand her desire for merger and takeover? Or is she finally beginning to lose it? Either way, its contents are now safely stowed in the vaults of her high-street bank.

I long to talk with her about other things. My life, for starters. But it always comes back to paper. Could I write a letter? Check a form? Countersign one legal document and safeguard another? If my father sought to forestall death by seeking refuge in his childhood, my mother appears to be counting on wearing down the grim reaper with wall-to-wall bureaucracy: there will be contracts to sign and witness; t's to cross and i's to dot; stamps to buy; and photocopies to be made and sent to solicitors and trustees. The world she leaves behind her will be ordered. Having struggled to make her mark by other means, my mother will have it stamped regardless.

I do appreciate that all our fussing with paper is a way of exporting our relationship to a safe bubble world where nothing can ignite. Here, amid the bookkeeping, we transact a symbolic exchange of trust and forgiveness, like dignitaries from warring countries meeting in neutral territory to sign an entente cordiale. It is our way of affirming that in spite of our myriad differences and our many spats and disagreements—extending back through a fiery past in which my mother's Middle Eastern traditions were continually pitted against my Western aspirations—we are contractually bound together by blood. And in the annals of loyalty, blood trumps everything.

The story I want to tell her is another peace offering. My mother understands intuitively the way stories forge bonds that sustain us, in that the older she gets the more she feeds on stories from her youth, told and retold in order to bind up and bridge the intervening years. But the trick works both ways, and this particular story pays forward. It is a modern-day Aesop's fable that might be called "How the Woman Got Her Menopause." It begins like this:

Menopause is a very rare thing among living beings, and for many hundreds of years it was little understood. The women who experienced it said almost nothing about it, save for in nervous whispers, and then they only whispered it to one another. Sometimes they bowed their heads in shame, letting gray-streaked tresses fall across their faces like veils, before they scuttled off to dusty corners where no one would mind them. Or they dragged their heavy limbs up hills, looking for sunbaked rocks they might lie on, there to shrivel up and desiccate in peace. Nobody much missed them, since hardly anyone noticed they had disappeared.

In the whole of the animal kingdom only three species of mammal experienced the menopause, and in all those species the no-longer-fertile females went on living into very old age. These were humans, orcas, and short-finned pilot whales. But still the women felt terribly alone, since their closest land-dwelling cousins—the primates—never had to bid farewell to fertility.

There were rare exceptions: tired old zoo apes and test-addled lab monkeys would occasionally become incapable of breeding. But this reproductive atrophy was considered most likely a symptom of their captivity, like depression. Nor did anyone know if, like women, menopausal orcas suffered hot flashes, night sweats, irritability, insomnia, vaginal dryness, and weight gain. It was and is still a mystery. All the same, observers reasoned, even if orcas were asymptomatic, the question remained as to how something so apparently maladaptive as menopause could have ever evolved.

In Darwinian terms, and this is the lens through which most of the observers I speak of peered, menopause is an oddity that begs explanation. If evolution is a game of survival, its winners will be those individuals who secure their genetic legacy by producing as many offspring as possible. The no-longer-fertile are surplus to requirement. So why, over time, hasn't that blind executioner, natural selection, weeded out the postmenopausal females?

When menopause was once thought unique to humans, the argument most often tendered in response was that the long lives of postmenopausal women was an artifact of modernity—an example of the way civilization mitigates against nature's grain to produce "monsters" (biology, reader, is as guilty as any other discipline of naked misogyny). But then the discovery of menopause in orcas in the last decades of the twentieth century invited a differently textured kind of thinking.

At this point I know that I will have captured my mother's attention, for although she would never call herself a feminist, she recognizes when she's being sidelined.

Orcas have evolved complex social structures that are fundamentally matriarchal, so that instead of merely rearing her young, a female orca, her breeding life behind her, will remain on hand to support adult offspring, improving their chances of survival by helping them compete for resources and dominance. Often, it is the female elders who lead their pods on a hunt. So dependent are the adult sons in particular on the aging mothers that, should she die, they are far more likely to die themselves. Fourteen times more likely, according to an international team of scientists who have spent long years studying orca populations in the North Pacific.

Humans, whales, and other long-lived species—elephants, arctic terns—are what is known as K-selected. The term refers to an evolutionary strategy first described by the sociobiologist E. O. Wilson to explain the trade-off between quality and quantity as reproductive goals. R-selected species, such as insects, rodents, and bacteria, are reproductively profligate; they produce many multitudes of offspring but then demonstrate almost no interest in rearing them. Odds are most of these offspring, left to fend for themselves, will die young; but because R-strategists produce so many, a few will survive into adulthood and begin reproducing themselves, thereby perpetuating the gene pool. K-strategists, by contrast, tend to be long-lived creatures for whom reproduction is difficult, lengthy, and energy-consuming. They produce very few offspring and these tend to mature late. But the parents invest mightily in each of them, often into adulthood, and often, as with orcas and humans, supported by elaborate social structures. For orcas and humans alike, this motherly investment extends well beyond fertility, apparently with nature's blessing.

This clearly adaptive function is how the woman got her menopause. Popularly known as the grandmother hypothesis, it was first outlined in a seminal paper of 1957 by the evolutionary biologist George C. Williams, a celebrated theorist of senescence.

Williams suggested that at some point in a mother's life it made evolutionary sense for her to stop producing children and concentrate instead on nurturing the children she already had. Menopause was thus a neat evolutionary switch that served to divert women from reproduction into long-term caring.

Williams also said that if the survival of genes was to some extent dependent on the survival of family groups, it was advantageous, in evolutionary terms, for mothers to continue investing in the care of their offspring's offspring—a phenomenon known as inclusive selection, or kin selection, which along with the concept of reciprocal altruism became the chief means by which evolutionary biologists explain the transmission of unselfish behavioral traits such as self-sacrifice, calculated risk-taking, and cooperation.

Support for the grandmother hypothesis has come from anthropological studies of remote hunter-gatherer societies, where social norms, unchanged for many thousands of years, are thought to offer clues about behavioral traits that count as adaptive. One such ethnic group is the Hadza, from northern Tanzania, a small, genetically homogenous tribe, whose members are among the last full-time hunter-gatherers in Africa. The Hadza live communally, in groups or "camps" of twenty to thirty individuals. These are mixed, generationally, and the Hadza rear their children together and share food; while the men hunt, the women forage. Post-menopausal women, it turns out, are a boon to the health of Hadza camps because they exert less strain on resources than reproductive females while continuing to forage for food. Meanwhile, the older women, the childless among them, are revered as bearers of cultural knowledge, memory, and experience.

My mother would relish this effortlessly layered story, from its orca beginnings to its tribal ends. Not only does it chime with a view of aging-female worth that reigns supreme in her personal universe, it girds it with evolutionary validation.

When she was growing up in the Middle East, inside a culture that looked upon Western individualism as suspect, my mother's operative unit, or unit of cohesion, was the clan. Urban and mercantile rather than rural hunter-gatherer, but a clan nonetheless. And within this clan, mothers and grandmothers held sway, leaving the outside world of work and politics and paid-for pleasures, such as smoke-filled coffee shops and gambling dens, to men. Clanship meant unity, solidarity, and cohesion to the point where the clan thought and moved as one. If any of its members were slighted or hurt, the rest protectively closed ranks around them; and if any behaved badly—strayed from a marriage, blundered into shady business deals—the entire clan would be tainted by their actions.

My mother was raised communally, by her mother most directly, but also by her grandmother, a proper old-school matriarch who knew very well her own power. Her religious education was entrusted to her pale-eyed, dreamy grandfather, while her social education was left to numerous aunts and uncles and their pinched-lipped spouses, and shored up by the cousins of the clan—all of them crowded into a topsy-turvy household, like the expansive brood belonging to the Old Woman in the Shoe.

The very building the family inhabited, in a Jewish suburb of old Baghdad, embodied the structural values of clanship. It was barricaded against the street and its traffic of otherness by a high-walled brick façade, while on the inside it opened up, and out, onto a light-filled courtyard, edged by a colonnaded corridor that offered shade from the burning sun, and it was alive with the sound of laughter and tinkling fountains. This courtyard was effectively the living room, the place people gathered to pore over the day's news and break bread together. In the evening chill, they would warm their hands around a brazier and tell one another stories, with the firelight crackling in their midst, and if the stars offered twinkling encouragement, one of the other-sighted among them would read the future in the spattered dark dregs of their Arabic coffee.

This was like something out of the *Tales of the Arabian Nights*, exotic, romantic, antique. Or so it struck me growing up in London, far removed in space and time from my mother's upbringing, and already corrupted—as it must have struck her—by the scourge of Western individualism. She was right, to a degree, since back then I never grasped that my mother's "we" was not the royal one that asserted prerogative but the collective "we" that stood for "us" and also made "us" a constituency of sorts.

Photographs that survive from that time always picture my mother, slight of frame and delicate as a bird, as part of a group: her nuclear family, her classmates, her clan. Shy and half-smiling, she's usually hiding behind an older relative or teacher. But if you look closely, you can see the life that resides in the eyes. Dancing, alert, intelligent, my mother's dark eyes betray her vital inner world. In another life—one that offered her more opportunity—she would have made more of herself, had a career, become a scholar, a lawyer, served her community: satisfied her active mind. As it is, her spirit found expression in family pride mixed with a spit of defiance.

My mother has lived in London for the largest part of her adult life, but her clan-held childhood is still her lodestar, her true north, the thing she returns to over and over as her life approaches full circle. Now a grandmother, and deeply invested in the urban survival of her three grandchildren (as per hypothesis), it is into their ears that she pours her tales of old Baghdad. I watch from the sidelines, observing my daughter getting swept up in the fairy-tale threads of the telling, enjoying her own state of not-quite-believing, and I suddenly remember how charged these stories were for me at that age, because I didn't want to be part of the clan: I wanted to belong to England. I can't help wondering if it is for my benefit that in these modern retellings my mother tries for a certain edge, lacing my grandmother's stern invigilation of unendurable lamp-lit sessions in needlepoint with overtones of foreboding, and dwelling on the mischief stirred up by her sister, whose inner fury seemed to channel the desert winds. Beneath my mother's scolding tones, it is clear that when it comes to her sister, she wishes she could have been so bold.

In Middle Eastern cultures, women are allotted the kind of prescribed roles that Western women, myself included, despair of. They are raised to be dutiful daughters and pliant wives, while everything they might want for themselves—careers, independence, education, travel—comes second or third, or never. Even the willful sister, my late aunt, crumpled under societal pressures to conform, her turbine energies dying on the breeze. Only when women are widowed or postmenopausal do such societies permit them to be simply themselves, and although this freedom arises perversely, since widows, spinsters, and postmenopausal mothers are essentially beneath notice, it is still freedom, nonetheless.

* * *

My mother never talked to me about menopause. But I remember her zooming around on HRT full of a gleeful energy. She would tee up errands that stretched from dawn till dusk and then tick them off with gusto. She was the archetype of Margaret Mead's "zestful" postmenopausal woman, motoring through her days, congratulating herself on how much she'd gotten done and tsking over her failures. And she did get an awful lot done. She was the only driver in the household and the only cook. The household help and the gardener were answerable to her. She paid the bills and oversaw the finances, while my father wafted about being "creative." Without her to ensure that his business remained on the right side of debt, I hate to think where we'd have been.

I've never encountered anybody less interested in process than my mother, quite possibly because process (like that tricksy individualism) invites introspection, and she believes that introspection is at root self-indulgent—as frivolous in its own way as a package of spa treatments. She believes instead in goals. Her realities are the concrete realities of the external world: this tree, this car, this shopping list. Or this showdown that needs to happen with the plumber, the local council, the traffic warden. Catch her fresh from such argy-bargy and she is engorged with satisfaction, glowingly gratified that such important duties have been properly discharged. Pausing to reflect on menopause, amid all this activity, would have been unthinkable.

"I don't care what you do, but don't ever put me in a home," she says whenever the subject of The Future comes up between us. So consistent is this plaintive cry it is practically a holy commandment. The subtext is quite clear. While Western individualists might enjoy their own company, might indeed revel in their independence, wishing ultimately to island themselves unto the end of their days so as to leave behind the lightest footprint and not burden anyone, she, my mother, desires no such thing. To untether oneself from the world and gently float off into the twilight—how could anyone want that? No, my mother's group-minded hope is that I acknowledge just one bond of clanship: that revered family elders, after a lifetime of serving others, might in old age fall back upon the care of their children. This is her due. Payable in arrears in exchange for the duty of care she met in raising us. It is the single most important thing on my mother's late-life to-do list, and she would like to see it definitively ticked.

While a horror of being tossed on the scrap heap is at one level completely understandable, it is compounded in my mother by the legacy of clanship. Her brain could never compute, for example, how a woman might survive d-i-v-o-r-c-e (a fate so unmentionable it had to be encoded). Should this unspeakable catastrophe—this excommunication—happen to befall the unlucky parents of my childhood friends, she would be stumped not just for words but basic comprehension. There were no points of empathy by which she might enter the woman's predicament; and it was always a predicament, for it was beyond my mother's ken to see how any woman might actually welcome so dangerous an uncoupling or view divorce as a relief and liberation. As with divorce, so with old age: both are a kind of abandonment.

The scrap heap continues to loom symbolically large for my mother in spite of my repeated assurances that she'll not in fact end up there. Like the bogeyman or the grim reaper, its ghoulish specter springs from the shadows at the merest wobble in her reasoning. Hers is a twilight fear, not quite real but not so easy to dismiss as

immaterial either. Over time I have learned that in the half-light
and shadow play I am best off assuaging any lingering trepidation
with a finger-wagging threat of "I'll put you in a home." This, for my
mother, is like flipping the brights on. It is high comedy.

There must be legions of women who, like me, put a certain faith
in the chain of transmission by which women are meant to hand
down knowledge to one another, mother to daughter, even when
their better judgment tells them that things seldom work this
way, that the chain isn't well oiled enough, or the links are bound
to break. When my own mother was going through menopause,
no one really talked about it (they called it the Change, for good-
ness' sake). But the truth is that I was unlikely to have listened even
if they had. Barely out of university, rudderless and devoted to
the joys and miseries of youth, I had disappeared down a well of
self-absorption. The little interest I evinced in my mother's experiences precisely matched her disincentive to share them.

Looking back, now that I am avid for her confidences, my
mother claims that she hardly noticed any deep tectonic rumblings
beneath the surface of her life. Certainly she didn't question cultural norms around menopause—Western ones now—that pushed
women off center stage once they'd passed fifty. She subscribed
instead to the baton-handing notion of succession. Even today,
she remains deeply suspicious of the me-centered revolution
engineered by the baby-boomer generation—the generation that
succeeded hers and then remodeled the political landscape: the
generation that, with the help of Gail Sheehy and Germaine Greer,
dragged menopause, slumping and hunchbacked, out of its shame-
filled hole and made it something to reckon with.

Curious to learn how my mother felt about the prevailing cultural trend of styling fifty as the new forty, and forty the new thirty, while insisting that you are only as old as you feel, I asked her. She guffawed. She turned eighty-three this year, and in the face of her ongoing struggles with mobility, memory loss, unpredictable plunges in blood pressure that send her reeling off-balance, and regular, if episodic, bereavement, she cannot see how eighty, in its turn, could possibly qualify as the new seventy. It was good to find something we agreed on so easily. And we have had our scares, to be sure. Horror moments after midnight when the phone rings, buzzing me into gut-churning wakefulness, and I have to race to her side because her bed feels as though it is yawing and pitching like a ship on the high seas. She retches, but nothing comes up. I fetch tissues and coax her into drinking water. Then we wait, sitting quietly together on the edge of her bed, holding hands under the waxing moon—one middle-aged woman and one old one, feeling the fragility of life and absurdly grateful to have each other still.

It is a popular fallacy that as a species we are living longer. It simply isn't the case. In most countries life expectancy continues to hover around the late-seventies mark (not far off the psalmist's "three score years and ten"), and in developing countries it is much lower. Yet, almost without exception, the popular literature on aging claims that thanks to better medicine and healthier diets, we are all living lengthier lives. Census figures are liberally quoted. Projections of how the ranks of the elderly will soon swell, freely offered. And all around sighs of gratified relief can be heard rising amid the rustle of statistical screeds.

A glancing acquaintance with census figures appears to confirm the good news. However, census findings are deceptive. The UK census of 1871 (the first of its kind) found, for example, that life expectancy for men averaged around forty-four. This seems shocking to us, brutal, unnatural, and since practically no one dies at forty-four these days, it seems reasonable to conclude that we are indeed living longer. After all, haven't we managed to get the upper hand on fatal diseases? Improved our living conditions, and successfully spread our wealth? Yet these social and cultural gains count for surprisingly little; as soon as you subtract infant mortality from the census equation, male life expectancy in 1871 instantly shoots up to a very contemporary-looking seventy-five.

Life expectancy is a function of genetics. Its span is a species-constant given. It should not be confused with life extension, which is a would-be science of longer living, with tendrils sunk deep into turbo-charged vitamins and vistas populated with shining visions of the frontiers of nanotechnology that owe more to science fiction than fact.

At eighty-three, my mother acknowledges that she's into penalty time, like those statistical outliers who live beyond ninety and one hundred and skew popular perceptions of this ultimate numbers game. For this particular demographic, each new year that arrives really is a gift—a mathematical one. Nor am I under any illusion about where I stand at fifty. It is an actuarial near certainty that I will have passed the halfway mark of my life and, very likely, Jung's high-water mark, too. From now on growing older will be less about clocking up the age I have arrived at than about counting down what is left. At fifty, I will be over the hill. Ahead of me, just as I am able to take command of the view, the incline runs downward. And it doesn't end well—although I do appreciate that the tenor of the journey (bumpy or smooth? vista-rich or thickly wooded?) will be largely up to me.

The calculus of aging aside, it is fair to say that medicine *has* helped us live healthily for longer. Hip replacements, cataract operations, pacemakers, arterial stents, blood-pressure medications, bolder cancer treatments, and assorted other add-ons, plug-ins, implants, or cures have meant that most of us now sail rather than hobble through our sixties and seventies. This is grand. It suggests progress.

Future interventions look more promising still. American evolutionary biologist Michael Rose is in the vanguard of research into gerontology, where he utilizes the latest findings in gene therapy and enzyme systems to experiment with postponing cellular aging. In his book *Methuselah Flies* (2004), Rose reported incredible results in extending the lifespan of fruit flies that he had selectively bred for longevity. At the time, he believed that his antiaging manipulations in rodents and fruit flies might scale up. But he has since changed his mind. Over the past decade he has come to believe that slowing the aging process is the best that we can do. His clarion call these days, which is that gene therapy should focus on the human "healthspan"—on life enhancement rather than life extension— appeals to me.

The scenario that Rose and his colleagues at the University of California, Irvine, envisage is that we remain fit and healthy throughout our seventies and early eighties, perhaps even longer, after which point we deteriorate with merciful alacrity. This step process seems to allow for a new topography of middle age that floats free of the number line, and that addresses what constitutes quality of life, but in a positive sense. Usually the term, applied to aging, connotes only an absence of suffering. If molecular genetics can help create a hiatus in the aging process, making the inevitable downward incline that much less steep, we might expect to have a very different psychic engagement with midlife. For if middle age is reconceived as a kind of plateau, there's no reason we shouldn't linger to enjoy the view. Or, for that matter, entertain approaches to middle age that occupy a more ambivalent zone, somewhere between my mother's unquestioning (if stoic) acceptance and the baby boomer's valiant, if wrongheaded, denial. Surely we can improvise attitudes that offer greater practical utility and hope?

I am exercised, as months melt away to weeks ahead of my turning fifty, by the extent to which biology is destiny. When I look in the mirror, I am struck by how much I seem to resemble one parent or the other. With my hair longer, I'm the spit of my father, jowls and all, but then as soon as I crop it, I morph into my mother. I am not talking about passing resemblances here, the way I've noticed how entire visages belonging to various relatives will sometimes drift across my daughter's face at odd, fleeting moments, like some rippling CGI effect. I am talking about virtual possession. Features cut according to a precise mold and then solidly fixed. Expressions that I had uniquely pinned to my father or mother, seemingly grafted from their faces to mine. Since when, I wonder, did I begin ceasing to look like myself?

As with so many aspects of midlife déjà vu, it is difficult not to feel that in aging you are stepping into already worn shoes. But what about the paths I choose to follow? Are these already mapped out for me, too, like some kind of genetic road map, origami'd into my brain from birth and only now sprung free?

In times past I would have reacted to such worrisome suspicions with great energy, batting away my parents' modeling of middle age with extreme examples of how to do it differently. I would have hauled studies off the library shelves to prove that in Indian cultures, no less, menopause grants women a kind of sovereignty. Hindu women can enter temples, for instance, and participate in sacred rituals once they are past ripe, and they are cherished for their life experience, too. And there would have been much affirmative finger-jabbing directed at various long-necked bluestockings who found their own quirky paths through midlife, carefully molding themselves to fit their forward-looking social agenda.

Nearing fifty, however, I am well aware of the limitations of cultural appropriation. I know that borrowing is not the same as owning. It's why I am so dubious about the idea of becoming a Buddhist, the better to weather American consumerism; or about growing a jihadist beard to signal cross-cultural solidarity or political disaffection. Besides, I am less interested in off-the-peg alternatives, or ready-made options for living that I might try on for size, than in searching for paths that are both different *and* authentic. I am after explorations, meditations, experimental sorties. I'm looking for tightrope-walking ventures into middle age with no guarantees of success.

At a hair shy of fifty, I know that only this sort of open-ended searching leads to finding, and that finding leads to having.

Teeth

OVER BREAKFAST MY HUSBAND IS ADAMANT: MILESTONE BIRTH-days require marking. I grunt in reluctant acknowledgment, sleep still cloying at my brain. Wrapping my fingers around my coffee mug, I wonder if I am to be harangued into doing something. "Get a caterer in," he says, "so you won't have to slave." He wants to save me laboring, wants my birthday to be a day of rest. But he is also provoking me. He knows that I am allergic to outsourcing any-thing to do with the home—my kingdom, inviolable!—and that certain kinds of slaving, cooking for people for example, give me a votive satisfaction. He is urging change on me, tempting me to break form. I tell him I'll think about it and we let the subject drop.

Secretly, I have been logging the ways in which people around me are choosing to turn fifty, turning them over in my mind and taking a mental sounding. I note, admiringly, that one friend has gifted himself three weeks off work so that he might walk the route of the Thames from its source in Gloucestershire, near where he was born, to the river's Essex estuary, close to where he now lives with his partner and daughter. As a metaphor for growth and expansion it is difficult to think of anything more topographically apt. He is packing a portable tent and looking forward to sampling the local beers en route. For him, the experience will be elemental.

Another friend embarked on a solo journey to Santiago de Compostela along the route used by the pilgrims of old, from Saint-Jean-Pied-de-Port in France's Basque southwest, tracking westward across northern Spain. She, too, walked, taking more than two months to cover some eight hundred kilometers, stopping to talk to people along the way and to drink in medieval churches. But mostly her idea was to dwell with herself. Reaching Burgos, roughly the halfway mark, she learned the symbolic pilgrim's lesson of how you cannot move forward if you are carrying too much. "Everything started to change in Burgos when I posted half my belongings back home," she wrote to me later. The swollen knee that hampered her progress could not be so easily set aside; and so instead of arriving in Santiago on the day of her birthday, as planned, she found herself walking in the hills through fog and mist until she reached the Cruz de Ferro, the iron cross where you leave something. For medieval pilgrims the cross had been a liminal point, the place they bid farewell to their old lives and moved into a new spiritual landscape; this, my friend realized, was her birthday present from the *camino*—the understanding that from now on she needed to travel light.

Pilgrimage seemed to be the common thread among my circle of acquaintances, with yet another friend venturing to a remote region of Zambia, to visit for the first time the hardscrabble farm where her late white-African mother had been raised. More proof, if I needed it, that so many of us spend the first halves of our lives running away from source, as determinedly as we can in many cases (like the rushing waters of the Thames barreling down to the sea), severing our connections along the way, only to embark on the second half attempting to find our way back, scanning for obscure points of reentry to spaces and places that have themselves changed.

I had already made my pilgrimage back to source, in my early forties. I had visited Baghdad for the first time during the temporary window of opportunity forced open by American and British bombs, and through which the market and its mother had gaily poured, trailing freelance mercenary fighters, telecommunications engineers, building contractors, loan sharks, and truckloads of Eastern European–made cars. Baghdad was, for a short while, and in the gung ho parlance of the day, "Open for Business." I was transporting my own contraband in the form of packages of vacuum-sealed kosher meat; stuffed into the zippered inner pockets of my suitcase, these were intended as calling cards for when I tracked down the last Jews of Iraq. At the time, just twenty-two were left, sorry representatives of an abandoned but once sizable community, of whom I met roughly half (and among whom, had events taken a slightly different turn, I might have counted myself). Now there are none.

I wrote about that journey at length, effectively tying the loose thread of myself back into history's weave, and now I was ready to move on. If anything, what I desired from fifty was to feel more at home where I was. In my skin, my marriage, my city, my house, my life.

This was an ambition whose scale I didn't dare underestimate given that my overwhelming feeling in so many aspects of my lived reality was a sense of rupture and dissolution. It seemed to me that if I was looking to fifty to show me how to make peace with myself, then a pilgrimage was not for me. I didn't need a destination or even, when it came to it, a celebration. I was after a rebirth. Not the rebirth beloved of self-help gurus, mind, which demands that we visualize exquisitely plumed birds rising up from blackened cinders, but something less showily transformative and more cellular; a coming together, or making whole, of the disparate parts of my liminal self, a reformulation of old elements according to a new arrangement: something akin to an invisible revolution.

The writer Colette, frizzle-haired, feline, and as exuberantly pro-lific in life as in words, was fond of viewing each radical new phase of her existence as a rebirth, or *renaissance*, as if each brace of books she wrote in tireless back-to-back jags, or each marriage whose road had ended, was a small death—as if, in completing them, she had expended herself.

With the exception of a singular moment in her late fifties when she made a project of herself, consciously moderating her drink and diet so as to lose weight (Colette was always heavy, but for the brief spell in which she tackled herself, she shrank to something like svelte) and signing up for the whacky rejuvenation procedure devised by Hélan Jaworski—a fashionable quack from Poland who administered blood transfusions to middle-aged matrons, where the donors were attractive young women—outside of this, Colette's rebirths were fundamentally symbolic. If Jaworski's treatments improved her vision and increased her vitality, or so she claimed, her symbolic rebirths touched her soul. Through them she refreshed herself, showed the world a new face, made a new peace with her past (her mother, in particular), trialed novel forms of writing, or embarked on an adventurous life journey with some new young lover, of whichever sex happened to tempt her.

Colette led an extraordinary twentieth-century life, even for someone as willfully unconventional as she was, traveling far from her bourgeois Burgundian roots under some primal propulsion to escape from, and yet impress, her ambitious mother, Sido. She began to write under the tutelage of her first husband, Henry Gauthier-Villars, a bumptious and controlling character who nevertheless dazzled the young Colette with his raffish urbanity. Under his name she published her wildly popular and quietly salacious Claudine novels. But the protégé soon outgrew the master. In 1906, Colette left "Willy" to go native among Paris's bohemian set, embarking on a career as a music-hall artiste and dabbling in a high lesbianism—a period of her life she captured in *La Vagabonde* (1910). My favorite photographs of her—kohl-eyed, bow-lipped, and dressed like an Oriental concubine—date from this period. They attest to how well she looked the part, even if the critics judged her better suited to the page than the stage. Colette was in any case impervious to their attacks; helplessly drawn to the spotlight, she continued to tour and perform whenever she needed a breath of inspiration-restoring air.

With the publication of her two Chéri novels in 1920 and 1926, Colette became a household name. Her fame was monumental. International. But she was never entirely comfortable being hailed as "France's greatest woman writer." Certainly she played up to the sobriquet, thinking it required her to behave outrageously or presumptuously, especially when there was an audience to entertain. Yet having reinvented herself so many times over, it proved just as easy to slip the weighty mantle; and then she often sought refuge beneath a persona that was just as false, that of the Burgundian wise woman, sweet, provincial, and ever ready with a recipe for furniture polish, orange wine, or quince jam, or for preserving linen.

In 1927, at the age of fifty-four, Colette channeled her ongoing commitment to rebirth into an austerely slim and yet voluptuously written novel titled *Break of Day*, in which she charts the adventures of a regally content middle-aged woman who is also called Colette. This semifictional Colette has taken up residence in a small cottage on the Provençal coast, where she intends to devote herself to her pets and her garden. At the same time she has determined, once and for all, to renounce love: "This is the beginning of a long rest between myself and men," she says. And again: "I have paid for my folly, shut away the heady young wine that intoxicated me, and folded up my big, floating heart." Her avowal is a choice, and a positive one at that; however, this being Colette, you're not quite meant to believe it. I have come to admire Colette more and more over the years. As a student I found her baroque language forbidding and also desperately old-fashioned, although I recognized her economically independent female characters—sybarites, actresses, widows, beauties (many of them women of a certain age)—to be mold-breaking, no matter that they were generally doomed or self-dooming. Reading her now, I see how wrong I was. Her writing is lush, nuanced, and often ironic. Her understanding of human nature is bristlingly fine-tuned, her modernity, extraordinary and unexpected.

Break of Day is an exultant piece of writing, a joyous paean to the simple life and the pleasures of solitude. It opens with its narrator marveling at the serenity she has found in her little country house and kitchen garden, in the company of her cats and dog, and with a hint of that "merciful moisture" promised by the coming rain—the "healing rain"—perpetually hanging in the air. A warming vision of a maternal ghost in an old-fashioned dress of blue sateen, filling watering cans on the edge of the well, completes the enchantment. Colette rhapsodizes over this "sweet entice-ment, this provincial spirit . . . this innocence," asking, "Isn't all this the charm of declining years?"

Very quickly, however, you realize that you are not dealing with someone even remotely in decline. This fictional Colette is sufficient to herself. She bathes in the sea, bronzing her skin and crisping it with salt; tends her tangerine trees, mulching them with succulent seaweed quilts; writes furiously on paper "the color of daylight in the dark"; and rests, pulling her mattress onto the terrace to bare herself to the elements. At the end of each day she sets a single place at the shady table under the wisteria, where she might enjoy a clinking bottle of wine drawn from the well, where it has been cooling in the musky dark.

That she is "merely alone, and not abandoned" in her solitary routine is something her Parisian friends struggle to grasp. Sophisti-cates one and all, they exclaim when they visit, "Oh, what a paradise!" But then they return to the city secretly totting up all that Colette lacks. They understand nothing of the "late-discovered riches" she has found within herself in this sun-soaked spot—still less, her "con-nivance" with the natural world around her that springs to life on practically every page in the book, fluttering, crawling, slinking, creeping, rattling, sawing, and squawking, as though Colette had retired not to the coast but to the rain forest or jungle. That visceral, brute animal force is something Colette identified with so strongly, both in life and in prose, that whenever her husband chanced to find her consorting with a furred or feathered friend, a fanged or clawed companion, he'd confess, "I feel I'm being indiscreet."

But Colette's sensuality is not confined to her relationship with animals. A love triangle is brewing under the southern sun, in which the virginal Hélène Clément, "pungently blonde" but "galumphing," and a terrible painter (one who tries too hard), is smitten with Valère Vial, a proud and private man who is an upholsterer by trade but nurtures the soul of an artist, and who also happens to have rented a tiny cottage down the road from Colette for the duration of the summer. Colette endeavors to play matchmaker between these would-be young lovers, but not, it turns out, on Hélène's behalf, rather her own, for in pushing Vial toward Hélène she is attempting to deflect the passionate upholsterer from an undying attachment to herself.

Or, half-attempting. Much of the time, Colette flirts outrageously with Vial, admiring his "bare body, polished by sun and salt," his "bronze arm" and "Egyptian shoulders." They eye each other attentively, in and out of company, and she is never shy of setting her hand "caressingly" upon his bare chest, whether to stay his desire or to stir it. In all this, Colette is knowing. Her hand, she says, "proclaims my age"; it is "burnt dark brown, and the skin is getting rather loose round the joints and on the back." Still, it is a hand good enough to create mischief!

The first time Colette touches Vial in this intimate way, they are together in her garden, grilling the "broken joints" of "plucked and mutilated chickens." Ever the coquette, Colette asks Vial to tie her apron at her back. Then, over the smoking animal flesh, she announces that next year she'll become vegetarian: "When one stops liking a certain kind of cannibalism, all the others leave of their own accord." This year, she says, rather pointedly, she's too hungry. Vial, you sense, is being granted a way out. He can leave Colette now, nurse his wounded ego, and attend to the pining Hélène or else stay and risk Colette's gobbling him up. Poor Vial. His fate is to be consumed, and thus annihilated, or else spat out.

In the event, it is the latter that comes to pass in a climactic scene staged over the course of a sleepless night, during which a mooching and sullen Vial confesses his "stillborn hope" to Colette. Colette is as flirtatious as ever, though she rejects him unequivocally as day finally breaks, its tentative, fragile new light bringing the illumination she craves. She explains to Vial, "I told you I was spending here a beautiful time of the year, but above all, a beautiful time of my life." This is a "new state," she confides, in which she doesn't always feel sure of herself. She cannot say for certain, for example, whether her great energy is because of her "new lightness or the remains of old fever." But she is committed to making a "clean sweep," to being "born again" and embarking on something she has "never done," to wit: "to live—or even die—without my life or death depending on love." Vial refuses to understand. Passive, pale, hollow-cheeked, vampiric, he mourns the loss of "color" that Colette brings to his days, fearing that without her he will be condemned to mediocrity.

At the end of this night of long knives, the depleted Vial is sent home regardless, while Colette, equally ragged with exhaustion, is brought back to herself by her material appetite, by the sour scent of peaches, forgotten in a bowl. "I bit into one and suddenly I was hungry and thirsty again for the round material world, crammed with savors." A few moments later, boiling milk, butter, and black coffee will "fulfill their healing office." You can almost see the blood returning to her cheeks, summoned by the influx of sustenance. Later come the healing rains longed for by our narrator at the start of the book, to complete the work of cleansing and rebirth.

This is a tremendous scene detailing the kind of relationship breakup we've all experienced: prolonged, exquisitely painful. It runs to many pages in the book, and you're never sure which way it will go. All the agonies of bringing something to life—a certain knowledge, a commitment—are there: the pains, in other words, of birthing. But there is also a philosophical weight to it, for in resisting the temptation of Vial, Colette not only recovers herself, she learns that she is more than enough, and also that she *has* more than enough. This is a form of wealth, an inheritance any of us might come into in midlife if we are clever enough to see it. And it is a wealth we might access via something as simple as boiled milk and butter.

In a powerful passage that might stand as a kind of manifesto for the novel and that is addressed, more or less, to the reader, Colette explains:

> I haven't taken too long to understand that an age comes for a woman, when, instead of clinging to beautiful feet that are impatient to roam the world, expressing herself in soothing words, boring tears and burning, ever-shorter sighs—an age comes when the only thing that is left for her is to enrich her own self.
>
> She hoards and reckons up everything, even to blows and scars—a scar being a mark which she did not carry at birth, an acquisition. When she sighs, "Oh, what a lot of sorrow He endowed me with!" she is, in spite of herself, weighing the value of the word—the value of the gifts. Little by little she stows them tranquilly away. But there are so many of them that in time she is forced, as her treasure increases, to stand back a little from it, like a painter from his work. She stands

back, and returns, and stands back again, pushing some scandalous detail into place, bringing into the light of day a memory drowned in shadow. By some unhoped-for art she becomes—equitable.

Reading this passage, I want to shout out, "Yes, I see exactly what you mean, and by the way, brava." A middle-aged woman is very much like a battle-scarred soldier. She has done her duty as a woman, and if she has done it well, she will have borne many wounds, for that is the nature of womanhood (very few of us get medals). And yet those wounds are to be cherished as defining, they have strengthened and built us, and once we own them, we need not weep over our catalog of hurts; rather, we must work with the raw material of our suffering and integrate it into newer, more mature, and more intricately sculpted selves. This, surely, is the very essence of rebirth.

In *The Coming of Age* (1970), Colette's compatriot Simone de Beauvoir, writing when she was sixty-two, would voice something similar, saying that life is "an unstable system in which balance is continually lost and continually gained." You shift this way, then that, aiming for poise but endlessly finding counterpoise, and you muddle through, unfazed, until, like the bubble on a spirit level, you settle into equilibrium. "Change is the law of life," wrote de Beauvoir.

Colette was the very opposite of de Beauvoir, playful to her earnest, evasive and intellectually inveigling to de Beauvoir's straight-shooting brilliance. The two women met at a house party in Paris once, and de Beauvoir came away from the encounter convinced that Colette hated her. What Colette thought of de Beauvoir is not on record, but she was always more comfortable with polite young women whom she could boss about and mother in her Burgundian wise-woman way. Colette delighted in shape-shifting (which would have unnerved de Beauvoir) and was always a step ahead of those critics who assumed that in her autobiographical fiction she was writing about herself. In *Break of Day* she scolded them gently: "Have patience; this is merely my model."

Those who see deceit in Colette point out that when she wrote *Break of Day*, she was far from renouncing love. She was deep into the heady throes of a relationship with the man who would later become her third and final husband, Maurice Goudeket, a Jewish pearl dealer of Dutch descent who was thirty-five when he began romancing the fifty-two-year-old Colette. Together they had bought La Treille Muscate (the cottage featuring in *Break of Day*) in 1925, and though Goudeket denied it vehemently, he was very likely the model for Vial. There are other "deceits" in the novel besides: Colette's mother, Sido, is characterized as a font of provincial wisdom and a nurturing übermum, when in truth Colette tussled constantly with her mother, frequently complaining to friends that Sido was insufferable. In *Break of Day*, Colette is charmed by children; in life, she wished to have as little to do with them as possible and practically cut off her own daughter.

Yet this question of veracity strikes me as a convenient decoy. For isn't a "model" merely the form we aspire to, that gives shape to our idea of perfection? If so, then perhaps when Colette models an equitable self in *Break of Day*, she is setting before readers a sort of avatar—an idealized self that embodies all the traits and inclinations we think our best selves are capable of achieving. On this view it hardly matters if her fantasy self is at odds with her person. What Colette desires, what she aspires to in midlife, is to emerge from her past as though "from a confused heap of feminine castoffs" and "escape from the age when she is a woman."

Midlife, to Colette, is about traveling lighter. This is why the extreme difficulty of renouncing what we love—men, meat, boring tears, and burning sighs—is the challenge that sits at the heart of this novel. Colette seems to be suggesting that renunciation is not to be equated with self-denial, but with an unburdening or unfettering that allows the spirit to soar.

This is monkish knowledge, revelatory, uplifting, but also counterfactual—and so we come back to the pilgrim's lesson. I find myself thinking here of Thomas Merton's poem "A Practical Program for Monks," which eulogizes the ascetic life. The poem is set out as a series of rather stringent rules, built around the regimen of sitting at table in a monastery—a time when monks come together to share a simple repast, a potato or a lemon, in Merton's rendering. Each monk has the same thing at the same time, like the ritual food that is blessed at a Passover table. Like sacramental food. Meager though these meals are, Merton is keen to tell us that they are sufficient:

Plenty of bread for everyone between prayers and the psalter: will
you recite another?
Merci, and Miserere.
Always mind both the clock and the Abbot until eternity.

Pray and eat, says Merton. Pray and give thanks. Pray and ask for mercy. Round and round the hours under the watchful eye of the Abbot, who seems to represent the Order's collective resolve. Merton is coming from a place that interests me intellectually; a Cistercian monk, Catholic mystic, and deep student of Buddhism, his faith is at once practical and transcendental. I approve of the philosophical mash-up, of finding singular ways to meld contrariness.

But on an emotional level my engagement with this question of how enriching mere sufficiency can be goes deeper still. It conjures the aesthetic pleasure of there being just enough and no more, as well as the thrill of jettisoning what's unnecessary, not just the junk that's easy to throw away, but the hard stuff: the stuff we cling to because it props up our false selves. It captures the tingling excitement of emerging unfettered from that confused heap of feminine castoffs.

Colette communicates very well how transcendent feelings might be grasped via renunciation: how going without is not about earning the right to indulge but about appreciating that everything that exceeds sufficiency is special. It explains her exuberant praise for the simplest gifts that nature bestows on her existence under the Provençal sun: the "blue salt shore," "the clink of bottles being carried to the well," a garden bursting with vegetable and animal joys. It's as if her eyes have been reopened.

Although in life Colette was famed for her greed—for gobbling up experiences, and lovers; for her all-consuming energy; her addiction to the stage and the limelight; her insatiable appetite (one of her biographers remarked that she didn't just eat éclairs, she "disemboweled them")—Maurice Goudeket insists there was another side to her.

The first evening they met, at the house of mutual friends, he relates how Colette seized an apple from the dinner table "and bit hungrily into it." Goudeket thought this part of her performance of being "France's greatest woman writer." But you couldn't invent a more symbolically laden scene, with Colette tasting the primordial forbidden fruit, analogue of the forbidden boy-lover—of which Goudeket was not her first. (In her late forties she had seduced her teenage stepson in a vengeful act against the philandering Henri de

Jouvenel, her second husband.) In old age Colette would give herself up to her voracious appetite, becoming unapologetically obese. But in his memoirs Goudeket writes of her "secret austerity." She took the greatest pleasure as a creature of her passions, he says, when she "put away from her what she most desired," adding that her greatest fear was that she could not resist giving everything away. "It is not the lukewarm who renounce most readily," he trills, adding that long before it ever occurred to him, it was she who decided when the moment had arrived "for our love to turn into friendship."

With *Break of Day*, Colette uncluttered her life further. The novel marked the start of her preference for the more stripped-down writing style associated with her later work, and for what would prove to be an enduring interest in autobiographical fiction, which is in some ways a literal unburdening, an offloading of life onto the page.

In France, the novel was published as *La Naissance du Jour*, or birth of day, thus aligning Colette's rebirth with the dawning of light, of revelation and of consciousness itself. But as her biographer Judith Thurman notes, the epiphanies of each new day get shrouded by the darkness of night, as we go back and forth and round and round, vacillating between growth and regression, blindness and lucidity, wholeness and fragmentation: a lifetime of continual adjustment. Because of this inevitable vacillation, this constant movement, this wave-particle imprecision, even Colette mistrusts the Colette in *Break of Day*. Perhaps that's why she's more painter than writer in treating her "model"—adding a touch here, then standing back, adding another there, and reviewing again. Perhaps what Colette means to suggest is that a woman in the process of rebirthing herself resists pinning down.

* * *

In middle age I am discovering that I care less about what other people think. I care less about material things, too—and about acquisition more generally. I am less hungry and more content. Gradually, I am shedding ballast and gaining buoyancy.

I have already experienced being the oldest person in the workplace, witness to the relentless forward thrust of younger colleagues—so fast and flash, yet sometimes so fixed. I know that studies of middle-aged brains repeatedly show that while younger brains display cognitive speed, older ones are more mutable, better at making connections and building bridges; and yet I also know how rarely this knowledge is applied. And so I salute the intellectual pizzazz of my young colleagues who forced a certain pace on me in surfing fast-moving developments in digital writing and publishing. I thank them for the chaff of high energy, like being on a high-speed train. I wish them luck and bid them adieu. I am relieved to register notes of difference between us.

There are other things I have gladly renounced besides the insatiable ambitions of youth. There is the quest for external markers of success, the wide playing field of sexual conquest, the idea that I will ever return to my peak fitness, the grievances I held against my parents for their inevitable failures, and more besides. I feel lighter for it. But also more grounded. I may not be the beacon of contentment that Colette succeeded in becoming (even fictively) in Break of Day—not the sovereign self of ideals—but my needs are leaner and my storehouse fuller. I trust my experience and expertise far more than I used to, and I better know my limitations.

I've come by much of this as a result of working through grief, mining my myriad losses in order to reach a deeper bedrock of identity. And so against the diminishments of aging that I have resented so sorely—the loss of vigor, organs, luster; the loss of a parent;

the loss of an unquestioning faith in possibility; the necessity of letting go of my former selves, some of them much cherished—1 can set the enrichment that derives from active renunciation: that monkish impulse that allows one to apprehend the more in less. And having shed, or sloughed off, so many (I now see them as futile) concerns, I find that I have more of myself to spare for generative schemes: for being neighborly and helping my mother, for volunteering my time at my daughter's school, and for community interests. For some years now the residents of Wilton Square have held a summer party for local residents, complete with pizza, face painting, and DIY music, and I've hurled myself into the administrative fray. I've also been campaigning: everything from trying to get traffic lights installed on dangerous crossings, to getting government to improve literacy standards. Having restored writing to a central place in my life, I find these days that all I think about is the reader: Are they with me? Do they care? If not, then I have failed them.

The not-so-much younger me would have actively spurned such generative concerns. I just didn't get them. When my daughter was in primary school, I had no idea how to talk to the mothers at the school gate, many of them high-powered career women, or they had been before they gave up work to focus on motherhood. By way of a direct transposition I found utterly bewildering, they would bring boardroom energy to the business of organizing cake sales and making bunting for the annual school fair. Vocal, vehement (and not a little terrifying), they'd argue the pros and cons in terms of bottom lines, cost-benefit analysis, and marketing strategies. This, I remember thinking, from brains that formerly exercised themselves advising MPs, running online fashion companies, and heading up architecture firms. These days I judge the mothers from my daughter's state primary less harshly for giving the best of themselves to a good cause. As a direct result of their bust-through-the-glass-ceiling standards, the school's summer fetes regularly turned profits many small businesses would admire.

That feeling of there being more of myself to parse out the less I dissipate my energies has gifted me a sense of deep pleasure in my own competence. After so many years of working at writing, feeling at worst a fraud and at best as if my long apprenticeship would never end and that I would never think of myself as fully fledged, I now take comfort at having mastered at least some aspects of the craft. I command a busy carousel of competing commitments that means I might spend one day editing a five-thousand-word essay I've commissioned for the magazine I work for; the next, teaching a life-writing class to a group of aspiring writers, some published, others not; and the next, I'll turn the volume of external demands right down in order to work on projects and commissions of my own. I now know, in other words, precisely how to balance what I need to give others against what I need to get in return.

Yet in spite of my recent generative endeavors, part of me would love to be sufficient to myself like the doyenne of La Treille Muscate. In my dreams, I envisage packing up shop and decamping to a sun-drenched spot where I might tend my garden and nuzzle my dog, read and write, hike up and down mountains, swim, task myself to learn Spanish or Italian, and exist for days on end off-line. My husband would be there like a shot. Tired of living in the gray city, overseered by the unrelenting grind, he is forever petitioning me with schemes of escape. But that particular enrichment will have to wait (for me at least; going on fifty-three, my husband says he's waited long enough, which makes for often difficult negotiations). But with a girl at school, a mother to look out for, and a self I have yet to cast off, still tied to conventional patterns of work—still subject to the "old fever"—I'm pinched between dream and reality. Still, I am mindful of how galvanizing change can be. Make one major move and whole wagon trains of unexpected experiences roll your way, much in that way that when you unburden yourself, you become more alive to the present moment.

All this I know. And, hopefully, all this lies ahead. For now I have fifty to attend to. Late in the day I decide to seize it, as Colette might have done. If twilight is going to be my time, then I shall string it up with fairy lights. The plan is this: I will invite family, friends, and neighbors to a birthday party at my house. I will not hire caterers. Instead I will cook, and I will make a glorious day of it. Alone, with the radio blaring, I will chop and dice and pare and fillet. I will mix and bake and marinade and grill. I will rearrange the furniture and sweep our small paved garden (it is the season of burrs, and they've carpeted the garden like a sea of prickly alien pods). I will tap my neighbors for extra chairs and a trestle table, and I'll make a last-minute run to the Japanese deli to buy some treats. I will labor because I choose to, and I will make of it a gift to the company I keep.

My daughter is wearing a blue lace dress and silver ballet shoes. The lights are low and the garden doors are open to the night. The dog is frantically eating up anything he can find that has fallen from people's plates, as though he's died and gone to scavenger heaven: fishy tidbits, bread crumbs, salad leaves (this is his lucky day). I'm surrounded by familiar faces, loved faces, and I am very aware of those that are missing. I think of them and send them a blessing. My daughter in her blue lace dress is holding a guitar. She will sing and play for us. She has chosen Cyndi Lauper's "True Colors"—a song whose lyrics make my tear ducts tingle. There is a hush as her honeyed voice fills the room, and my soppy heart swells with pride. Glasses filled with golden bubbles clink. Laughter and warmth abound and I am more content than I ever imagined I could be.

This is what I remember. And I will remember it always.

Head

On a warm summer's evening in July 2014 we gathered. Our chosen venue, the café beyond the Rose Garden at London's Regent's Park. Swooping on an outdoor wooden table, we clustered around it proprietarily, pulling over extra chairs to make up our number. We need not have been so precipitous. At 7:00 p.m. on a weekday the park was emptying. Abandoned deck chairs, stripy and cheerful, lay scattered among the lawns. Gaggles of texting teenagers drifted lazily toward the park gates, hijabs flapping on the evening breeze. Mothers with too-tired children, ice-cream smears on their faces, were heading home amid fits of crying and noncooperation. We had come to fill the spaces people left. Taking up occupancy on wonky folding chairs, we leaned in to our comradely circle.

We were six women in all, huddled around fifty like a statistical consensus on a graph, and brought together by another woman who wasn't present. One of us had come with pink fizz, another with a good bottle of wine. One brought olives, another arrived with punnets of strawberries and cherries, and fruit-flavored macaroons. It was to be a celebration of sorts, a nervous, high-hoped commemoration of our absent friend. Popping the cork on the fizz, we giggled as F pulled from a carrier bag half a dozen plastic glasses with separate plastic stems that screwed on. This was shaping up to be a DIY affair: a picnic, but at a restaurant.

"It must be against the rules to bring your own booze," said W.

"Perhaps it is," I said, "but this is important."

"Kirsty wouldn't have liked us breaking the rules, don't you think?" said F, testing out the feel of noncompliance. "She would have worried about it."

"Since we'll be ordering food in a minute, I doubt they'll mind," said T.

So the fizz was poured and the plastic glasses chinked, or clopped, as we toasted our friend Kirsty, dead now for exactly one year.

I had been dreaming about Kirsty. Dreams that felt tangibly real, in which she hovered near the ceiling of my bedroom, crosslegged like a yogi. Through her I could see the ridged cornice work, but that didn't seem to be of consequence. Instead there was an overwhelming sense of presence, like a concentrate, that penetrated my sleep so completely that I half-expected on waking to find the walls smeared with ectoplasm, *Ghostbusters*-style.

Garrulous and offhand, this diaphanous Kirsty was full of ideas and advice and jokey admonishments. Talking ten to the dozen and with great insistence, she opened up unseen perspectives on my problems, dancing lightly around them with a rapid-fire, singsongy ease, before swooping in for an acerbic kill. This usually began, *I don't see why you can't just* ... or *It's all very well him saying that, but* ...

Uncharacteristically, I was a silent partner in these transactions, an empty vessel into which my late friend poured herself unstintingly, like a genie of the bottle.

I told the Cavalry, for that is what our group now called itself, about these dreams, their urgency (their frequency!). From a cluster of loosely associated acquaintances in orbit around Kirsty, her decline and death had turned us into solid friends. We had got into the habit of exchanging information about her, initially because information was so hard to come by, but later as a way of inflecting things back upon ourselves, and so confiding my ghostly visitations came easily.

W asked if the dreams weren't upsetting. They weren't. They were warming, heartening even. The Kirsty Milne of my dreams, witty, astute, and teasingly provocative, felt more alive than ever. She was Kirsty squared. Kirsty to the max. She took my problems one by one and detonated them.

Far more disturbing to me were the bureaucratic hauntings. I would get the occasional e-mail in my in-box from a PR professional called Kirsty Milner, its arrival never failing to deliver an unpleasant jolt. And every so often LinkedIn would invite me to "connect" with Kirsty Milne, and some horror-house impulse would impel me to open the invitation, whereupon instead of the photographic portrait I was expecting to see there'd be a whited-out silhouette of a decapitated head.

F explained how at a social gathering a few weeks earlier she had been describing a holiday that she and Kirsty had taken together in Italy some years before. She had grown flustered upon finding that she couldn't recall many significant details beyond the clear lineaments of the trip. Kirsty would have remembered them, she said. But there was no way to retrieve those missing memories now. F would be the keeper of a half memory, something spoiled that would continue to decay with time. This is not the sort of loss we tend to think about in the ordinary run of things, but when your friends die, as my mother's generation knows all too well, they take their portion of your memories with them.

We munched our olives, green and meaty and salty, and we talked about what a good idea it had been to meet like this, because it had been a year, although it didn't feel like one: neither the speed with which it had elapsed, nor the perverse nature of what it marked—a black anniversary. And Kirsty so very much did not want to be forgotten.

By the end of an evening of reminiscence, stuffed with stories dating from before her illness and supplemented (as we replenished our supply of wine) by stories from the cancer years, it almost felt as if Kirsty was among us. Except she wasn't. So we decided to meet again every year, to hold an annual unforgetting.

The only symptom had been a cough, dry and mildly irritating. But it wouldn't go away. It had to be viral, she had thought. Or maybe it was something she had picked up from her husband, who had been traveling in Morocco for work. She didn't feel tired or achy, was sleeping well, and was perfectly able to concentrate on work. Kirsty had left journalism in her forties to pursue an academic career, and she'd harnessed all those years of writing to deadline to make fast progress. Now she was writing up a doctoral thesis that set out to track the shape-shifting means by which the sinful preferments of Bunyan's Vanity Fair, its trials and terrors, had morphed into Thackeray's parade of gilded consumerism and celebrity. Then she began to cough up blood. A series of rush-rush X-rays and bronchial biopsies was ordered, and the grim truth soon revealed: this was stage-four lung cancer. It was neither contained nor containable. Nobody talked about a prognosis, but the word *palliative* was attached to the word *treatment* from the very start. At home I googled endlessly. The rest of what would become the Cavalry did likewise, and we pooled our patchwork researches on symptoms, treatments, side effects, experimental drugs, combination drugs, alternative therapies, and oddball diets. It turned out that the life expectancy of someone in Kirsty's position might be as little as eight months.

As things went, and both for better and worse, Kirsty lived much longer, a little more than three years from diagnosis. But these were years of a radically new kind that I hope never to experience: borrowed time. Time that didn't by rights belong to her. Time that was pilfered from a future that disallowed the loan. Time that could be abruptly pulled from under her at any moment. It was angry, uncomprehending, and very often miserable time.

Throughout her illness Kirsty continued to work on her thesis, in spurts. It gave her a clear focus, but it also enlarged the world from an ambit that had become intolerably narrow. Although it is tempting to source this labor to her steel-capped single-mindedness, I'm not sure that this was its origin. I think it was born of love. Kirsty did not have children; instead the thesis was the thing she nurtured, and she was committed to giving the best of herself to the task of completing it even if that entailed making stark and difficult choices about what to cut out of her life.

I have some sympathy for this as a writer. A book demands an exclusive devotion: you have to disappear into it as you respond to its inner call, leaving people around you to wonder where you've gone. You are there but also not there. The healthy can juggle and just about traffic between these two states of presence, disappearing and reappearing at will. For the terminally ill it is too much to ask. Yet, at the time, I was unaware that Kirsty had simultaneously disappeared into an entirely different parallel world in search of a kind of belonging and camaraderie that her friends could no longer supply. That revelation was still to come.

What was apparent was that the effort her thesis cost her was practically superhuman. You could almost see her scrabbling as she tried to hoard up and hold on to her energies so that she might suddenly make a break for new shores, striking out with terrific bursts of speed (head up, keep breathing) while the strong undertow of the cancer kept pulling her back into the anxious, pain-soaked deep. Her everyday suffering doesn't bear cataloging.

But the thesis was finished, and now there is a posthumous book that can be ordered at the click of a keypad on Amazon.

At Vanity Fair has been published by Cambridge University Press in the very week that I am writing this. I summon it up, toggle over to *Look inside*, and I read. I am a little weirded out at having so easily obtained instant access to many thousands of words written by my late friend, and since I am looking for her in them, I cannot read them at face value, only as encrypted text. I am thrown by the fact the voice I encounter is not recognizably hers. It is filtered through the arch formality of an academic language behind whose stock turns of phrase I can feel her hiding, just out of reach. It is as if she were running behind the print on the pages, giggling and free, like the little girl I'd seen in photographs, bob-haired and tweed-coated, playing hide-and-seek with her brothers in the woodlands surrounding Glasgow in the 1960s. Now you see her, now you don't. Just as you think you've glimpsed her, she vanishes.

I read on, straining to locate the woman I knew amid the skeins of verbal camouflage. Because she is artful, I grow absorbed in the story. Losing myself in the fluidity of the telling, I even begin to warm to Bunyan's heavy-handed parable, which in her expert hands is transformed into something I want to read again, right now, with Bunyan suddenly a literary sophisticate who draws on and even subverts existing traditions of religious writing—he's preaching coded messages, toying with his blockhead opponents. Then all of a sudden I am pulled up short by the ring of something that seems indelibly hers: "material histories of the book take one only so far"; "a snippet of seventeenth-century nonconformity"; "a magpie mentality that prizes lists over explanations." Mad though it is, I almost feel as if I am being called.

I start to listen in more keenly. Before long, I can hear her coming through in practically every line, a ghostly presence furiously commanding the Ouija board, driving the argument first one way then another, marshaling ideas with a deftness that belonged to a fantastically sharp but also nuanced mind. I pick up her humor, warmth, and occasional impatience—especially with poor Bunyan and his lack of any comparable verbal panache. I hear her decisiveness and her compassion and her take-no-prisoners approach to intellectual purity, and I miss her all over again with a sharp pang of loss. With one click I am out of the book.

At first, Kirsty had wanted her friends around her as much-needed shock absorbers. She could rail against her bad luck (she had never smoked), rotten genes, and cruel fate and remain confident that we would stay close and buffer her against the menace posed by an outside world that had suddenly grown much more dangerous.

She was living in Oxford at the time. Her husband, H, whose work was in London, commuted back and forth. On days when he couldn't stay in Oxford, one of us six—it was Kirsty who first dubbed us the Cavalry—would be summoned to keep her company. We were told not to talk about the cancer, to tread sensitively, to let her lead the conversation. But cancer was all she wanted to talk about. She was desperate to contain it, as only talk could do (medicine having already fallen at that hurdle). But she was also wary of the power of talk, afraid its free-ranging ways would take her to places to which she wasn't yet ready to go. When this invariably happened, when our runaway banter unwittingly strayed and we'd hit up against these invisible walls, she would either clam up or leave the room—her pointed silence painfully conceding that words could not master this, this "thing," this clump of cells that kept outsmarting her quicksilver tongue.

Whenever I found myself alone like this, Kirsty having fled the room, I was eaten up with guilt. What exactly had I said to throw her? What word, or combination of words? Or perhaps it was something in my tone? The level of self-policing required to keep the temperature of the conversation just so took so much concentration—though I knew very well the subjects it was impossible to discuss: our mutual age and stage of life, and our (no-longer-shared) situation.

One time I trained over to Oxford to stay the night after Kirsty had begun a course of radiotherapy, with side effects that seemed to be immediate. Her fine hair, formerly a glossy Louise Brooks–style helmet, was falling out in sheaves. This was something that Kirsty knew very well, but she also contrived to not know it. I wasn't sure how to play it. The falling-out hair was so deliberately ignored. While I twigged soon enough that it was Never To Be Mentioned,

I became fixated with it. Each time Kirsty left the room, whichever room we happened to be in, I would grab the broom in a kind of panic, blood thudding in my ears, and sweep the evidence that could not be acknowledged off the floor and into the bin.

A memory. Kirsty moved back to London to save H the commute and be nearer her oncologists, and so there came a run of a couple of months when I would tube over to West London once a week to cook her an evening meal. She wanted idiosyncratic things to eat, depending on her mood: cauliflower, apples, cheese, Cadbury's chocolate (the expensive kind was held in great disdain), as well as specific salads from Marks & Spencer. There were long, dictatorial e-mails about what not to buy. I loved the whimsy of these orders, which seemed to suggest fancy and appetite and an interest in the minutiae of life—things one associates with good health. Happily, I would dash off to the supermarket on a mission and buy a selection of the requested items so that she could enjoy the feeling of having a choice, however small. But when it came to it, Kirsty could only equate food with sustenance (or pleasure, or sociability) in the abstract. The task of actually having to eat brought on waves of nausea, and most weeks I ended up pushing my offerings into the maw of a giant fridge so overstuffed from errands lovingly undertaken that it was practically warm.

Another memory. That first Christmas postdiagnosis, Kirsty invited us to see in the New Year with her and H in a rented cottage in Sussex. She had battled a severe pneumonia the previous month that had left her dependent on a nebulizer and, worse, feeling as if she'd already had a close brush with death, as though her hospital stay had been some kind of morbid dress rehearsal. Convinced that time was very short, she was determined to attend the Sunday service at the local parish church. Off she trundled, alone, which was her preference, a small huddled figure disappearing down the muddy lane, while the rest of us, who spent the morning walking up and down hills in unexpected sunshine, fervently prayed that she would find what she was looking for: comfort in the rituals of Anglicanism if not its articles of faith. At least that's what we thought she was looking for.

Later, she asked if I would put her in touch with a friend of mine, a wise woman priest roughly our own age. "How do you say good-bye to people you love when you don't believe you're going anywhere?" she'd said.

Shortly after that Christmas, Kirsty embarked on a new and uncertain phase of her life: she began living with her cancer as opposed to dying with it. The shift in thinking came courtesy of a life-prolonging drug that she began taking that winter, a still-controversial enzyme inhibitor that works by blocking signals prompting the manufacture of particular proteins that, in turn, encourage cancer cells to grow. This new drug regime—merciful, joyful—also coincided with a retreat from the world. Kirsty just turned her back on it all. Her friends included. The Cavalry—so close to her, and now to one another—was cut off at the pass. Or rather, we suddenly found the pass barricaded with large boulders that all our love and effort could not budge.

Out in the cold of rejection I had plenty of time to reflect on things. How did I think I would fare against such a death sentence? I asked myself this question over and over. Kirsty was just forty-six when she was diagnosed, forty-seven when she bulletproofed herself against the world, as though stepping into some kind of sci-fi pod. Would I, would my husband, would W, or F or R, or J or T, cordon ourselves off that way? Wouldn't we want to surround ourselves with loved ones? Wouldn't we long for comfort? My husband had an insight that helped. He suggested that in dying people become more, not less, themselves. All their traits become magnified. His explanation struck home with me since I knew that Kirsty had always found protection in silence. I let her be, though it wasn't my choice.

Occasionally a phone call would arrive out of the blue and wind me. I'd sit apprehensively on the stairs and we would chat as if everything were normal. Wiser to her ways now, I let Kirsty lead us in conversation over the eggshells, terrified of making a misstep. She told me she had taken up swimming a few times a week, and that apart from experiencing shortness of breath, she relished being in the water; that she and H had spent some time at H's uncle's house, within sight of the sea near Arisaig, in the western highlands—a spot of magnificent beauty and calm that had made her heart sing. . . . Water again. She also said she was considering moving back to Scotland toward the end of her life and that this thought gave her some portion of peace.

I now see that these phone calls were part of her survival strategy. In facing her death with tremendous bravery but also an implacable fear she valiantly attempted to find ways to live from day to day that might hold this contrariness in check. Often she would fail, and then she was prone to dreadful self-castigation when she ought to have been shaking her fist at fate. But then, sometimes, something as simple as a normalizing phone call might just effect the trick of reconciling these split selves, just for a moment, a tick, a beat, and then she might inhabit a self who could tell stories and make plans. And sometimes a moment such as this, pushed out to its fully authored potential—rescued from the abyss!—was sufficient.

With no future to look forward to, Kirsty was obliged to reinvent what we understand by continuity. It is a version of what we all have to do in middle age anyway, but in acute form. She stopped reading books and seeing movies, for instance, because she was unwilling, as she once explained to me, to commit to duration. When I reminded the Cavalry of this allergy to books and movies, T e-mailed me saying that she had always understood Kirsty's sudden phobia in terms of her wish to avoid anything that had an ending. Now I wondered about this: Was it duration or endings that traumatized her? Or was it more that in her case the end simply contaminated everything?

Certainly when it came to the long periods in which she somehow couldn't bear to see her close friends, duration was the problem: the fact that we had tomorrows. Though Kirsty was far too sensitive a soul to say so outright, I am pretty sure that she cut us off because much as we tried to inhabit her present—her artificially prolonged Now—we would inevitably slip up and refer to some upcoming plan or other, thereby betraying ourselves as beings who still lived inside Time.

In the vivid moments I spent with Kirsty, cooking for her, discussing politics, or massaging her hands or feet, I can recall with pointed clarity how my naked appreciation of being alive leapfrogged over so many other competing feelings and surged toward the forefront of my conscious mind. I was salivatingly grateful for my good health. Embarrassingly grateful. Whenever I left Kirsty, I would have firmly resolved to cut away extraneous things, to always act mindfully, to live fully cognizant of spending precious time in meaningful ways. I promised myself that from now on I would read with greater attentiveness, life being quite literally too short not to savor every word. I would eat with patience and joy. I would relish the world around me, always: the quality and shape and color and sound of rustling leaves; the weight and tone and feel and import of something my daughter confided.

This longing to experience life as something bursting at the seams, something so intensely felt as to seem almost hyperreal, has application to aging. It is a version of the idea that the older you get, the less you take for granted. The simplest joys get rounded out, experienced to their fullest potential. But in midlife, that longing arises principally as a corrective to ennui—an insidious malaise that afflicts those of us lucky enough to take continuity for granted.

Of all the curveballs that midlife has thrown me, the least anticipated has been a species of ennui, nudged on by the overwhelming and oppressive sense that one has seen it all before, from the ravages of war, natural disasters, extreme weather, and political promises made then broken, to heartache, grief, joy, and fear. Sometimes the feeling is so acute that real life collapses to the flatness of a theatrical performance, and you (or at least I) feel like those disagreeable characters from *The Muppets*, harrumphing at the hapless players on life's stage from the lofty heights of their balcony seat.

And there are circles within the circles, too, when beyond history and the world of events you have to endure interminable rounds of routine recycling, of music, art, fashion, and culture. The older you are, the more often it seems as if things come around: "Why are we watching this?"—Statler and Waldorf again. Of course there is the retro thrill of dressing like your granny but giving the ensemble a contemporary twist, and the hit of nostalgia offered by, say, music sampling, or playing mind games against Shazam, and there's the faux-learnedness of knowing quotation. But when you've seen it enough times, even the friendly engagement feels tired. I used to think literature offered greater scope for invention, but too often I've picked up the latest title only to find that I've read the story before—often several times before.

The trouble with this looped cultural circuitry is that it creates the illusion that time is speeding up. You recognize familiar markers instantly, summarily tick them off, and move on. Weeks, months, even years, seem to slip through your fingers as more and more of life's richness registers as just so much déjà vu. As the biblical writer of Ecclesiastes famously complained, "All things are full of weariness; / . . . What has been is what will be, / and what has been done is what will be done, / and there is nothing new under the sun."

Kirsty, of course, could not afford the luxury of ennui. If anything, she relished the ritual joy of repetition, of underscoring, over and over, what really mattered to her. In those rare moments when she was able to sideline her fear, she did manage to live in the present moment, savoring the most ordinary (and most wondrous) of life's experiences: the taste of cheap chocolate, the pleasures of work, the feel of water on skin, the love of a good man. At her very best she imbued such moments with practically transcendent meaning.

Ritual is a clever ruse. Its repeated observances invoke a sense of time that is eternal and in which the acts we perform now, here, today, become, in effect, symbolic reenactments of intransient verities that belong to a higher plane of existence. If someone was looking to escape the severities of linear time, especially under the cosh of an enforced ending, then he or she might do a lot worse than to duck inside ritual.

Looking back now—now that Kirsty's book is so eloquent a testimony to her life's achievement—I try to make sense of her having reserved the best part of her limited energies for writing about *The*

Pilgrim's Progress and its terrifying vision of Vanity Fair, with its law courts set up in judgment, its sinful lords, cheats, knaves, and manifold punishments—all those illegitimate authorities we habitually treat as guardians of the truth. Bunyan quotes Ecclesiastes's words of warning: "Vanity of vanities. All is vanity!" None of these authorities, despite their instrumental allure, have any claim on us, says Bunyan. They are ephemeral things, distractions from what is real and good. *The Pilgrim's Progress* is such a religious text for an unbeliever to have dwelled with so intensely that I puzzle over it. Yet when I was asked to write her obituary for *The Guardian*, family members told me how as a precocious child, barely six years old, Kirsty liked to linger in the bathtub as the water grew cold because she didn't want her mother, reading out aloud to her from *The Pilgrim's Progress*, to ever stop. This book marked the whole course of her life, not just her death. It touched the very root of who she was. Toward the end of her life, its ritual rereading, perhaps more than anything else she might have done, signified continuity.

Kirsty had wanted an excerpt from Bunyan to be read at her memorial service, which she had a hand in planning. She selected the passage in which Christian and Hopeful, after a long and perilous journey, at last come within sight of the heavenly city. But there is one final impediment to their entering its gate—a river that is both deep and bridgeless. There is nothing for it but for the terrified pilgrims to attempt a crossing. Almost from the outset, Christian is overwhelmed by waves breaking over his head ("sometimes he would be quite gone down, and then, ere a while, he would rise up again half dead"). He cannot find any firm footing no matter the trying, and he panics, his fear giving way to a "horror of mind" in which he sees darkness all around. He has to hold fast to Hopeful and to somehow find within himself both courage and faith. He has to search for an inner calm amid the raging tumult outside him. This he succeeds in doing almost in spite of himself. He is drowning, yet he trusts that he will reach the other side.

In her book Kirsty will not be pinned down on what precisely Bunyan's many allegories refer to. Vanity Fair, she insists, remains mysterious and alluring because its referents remain fuzzy. And yet fording the river seems to have spoken to her clearly, as though it was figurative of her own journey through illness, her sinking and rising, her losing the ground beneath her feet; and if it wasn't emblematic of her being led, finally, through the gates of heaven, then perhaps at the very least it afforded her a safe passage through death's door.

I think about Kirsty often. I can conjure a lifelike mental image of her still, hear the timbre of her voice, the lilting pattern of her speech and her curt, triumphant guffaw: "Ha!" It sometimes feels as though she's never left my side—which is the point, because her absence means that she will not be aging alongside me. In losing a fellow traveler who should have shared being fifty with me, and fifty-five, and sixty-five, I have lost a touchstone and a yardstick; together we would have taken comfort in mirroring each other, not simply in terms of a wrinkle for a wrinkle, but in being able to stand face-to-face and trace the through-line back to youth. The two of us would be able to see what *hadn't* changed. In ten years time, or in fifteen, when the unreality of Kirsty's absence settles into a proper distance, she will seem perfectly frozen, like the cli-chéd Marilyn Monroe, sealed in memories and pictures, her words left behind in books, her essential essence canned and stored in the fading recollections of her aging friends.

The bigger lesson here is that one should not age alone, and I say this irrespective of how much I am drawn to Colette's ideal of regal solitude and monkish self-sufficiency. You need a cohort of peers to age alongside you. A cackle of crones, a cavalry! You need fellowship and you need parity. You need to be able to disappear into the ranks and not always stand out like a beacon of generational change. You need community and camaraderie and comfort. This is why I shall continue to meet with W and F and T and R and J every July.

Our reunions will be an unforgetting, yes, but also a pledge to move forward together.

What I am attempting to describe here is a horizontal sharing of knowledge and experience that cuts in a different direction to the mother-to-daughter transmission of women's secrets that we are more familiar with. Happily, it is egalitarian. There isn't one party who knows more than the other or has greater retrospective purchase on things. It also has something in common with clan-think, but where the family clan can be prescriptive and doctrinaire, my cohort of equals is as fluid as a Mexican wave. None of the generational calibrations that one has to make with mothers impedes communication between us, since twenty or twenty-five or thirty years is a distance that requires cultural bridging. But mostly, taking this bias-cut across time prevents us from having to go through a difficult rite of passage alone.

When Kirsty cut the cord that bound her to her friends, she took up with a new family of peers, online, at an organization called GRACE. Among this community, made up exclusively of lung-cancer sufferers, she could quiz doctors directly, compare clinical notes, and recommend to fellow sufferers courses of treatment, all without having to pretend anything else was on her mind. For three years Kirsty was an almost constant presence on GRACE.

She became known in the community for the pointed questions she put to experts, but also for the extraordinary kindness and sympathy she extended to fellow patients, as scared, depressed, and despairing as she often was herself, though you'd never guess at her own fears and qualms from her upbeat posts.

At GRACE, Kirsty chose the name Certain Spring, which she took from Laurence Binyon's Second World War poem "The Burning of the Leaves"—an autumnal poem about the dying world that nonetheless ends with hope eternal. From the world that was ours but that is no more, runs Binyon's poem: "They will come again, the leaf and the flower, to arise / From squalor of rottenness into the old splendour, / . . . Earth cares for her own ruins, naught for ours. / Nothing is certain, only the certain spring."

Until the end no one at GRACE knew her real name, but when Kirsty died, one of her brothers thought to let the community know a bit about their late companion. They were disconsolate. Messages and tributes poured in, raw and unedited. People were heartbroken, their howls of pain revealing a whole other river of sorrow that ran alongside the loss felt by her family and friends. At her memorial service, some of these tributes were read out, along with one or two of Kirsty's own posts on GRACE. Highly charged and extremely discomfiting, these readings returned the visceral agony of having to live under a death sentence to the meditative melancholy of the memorial. Listening to them was like being pinched all over by a thousand tiny hands. Yet the GRACE readings also stood as an acknowledgment of a cohort of fellow travelers who had helped Kirsty make sense of her illness in ways that the healthy never could.

As for the Cavalry, we clubbed together not long ago to dedicate a reading-room chair at Oxford's Bodleian Library to the memory of our absent friend. We were allowed forty-six characters to commemorate her, barely a third of a tweet. After a bit of toing and froing in which various suggestions were tendered and hotly discussed, we settled on the words *Kirsty Milne 1964–2013: Reader, writer, friend.* Googling an image of the chair now, I wonder how Kirsty would have liked sitting in it. It is elegant and curvy, to be sure, but it is not cozy, and Kirsty liked to inhabit a chair. She would climb into it, kick off her shoes, curl bare feet beneath her bottom, and burrow in. It was as if she wanted to meld herself to the fabric. As if she wanted to disappear.

Spine

I WAS ONE OF THOSE JEWISH SCHOOLGIRLS ENAMORED OF A
Christian assembly. Six hundred girls, crammed into a high-
ceilinged, many-windowed hall and aligned in neat rows, forty
deep, as though in church, all of us emptying our lungs into the
ringing atmosphere in passionate unison to the accompaniment of
a soft-pedaled piano. "Bring me my bow of burning gold / Bring me
my arrows of desire." We'd belt out Blake's poetry as though aiming
for glory, the volume of our chorused efforts amplifying the trans
gressive kick. The sound we made was forceful, rousing, and my
heart would vault as a knot of difficult and otherwise unexpressed
teenage emotions began to unfurl and rise up in me as if reaching
toward some celestial magnificence—"O clouds, unfold!" The
words, the mood, the hope, the joining of so many girls, their collective spirit melded into song: all of it was wonderfully crystalline.
What could be more pure?

Although "Jerusalem" was our official school hymn (and we sang many other melodic numbers besides, on a ration of one per day), our headmistress, a starchy relic from the Edwardian era, with the magnificent name of Miss Leslia Marjoribanks, had a favorite hymn of her own that she would regularly sneak into the assembly carousel. The hymn was as Edwardian she was. Written by the Anglo-Welsh composer Henry Walford Davies, it is neither tuneful nor uplifting; however, its long-sliding hum has never left me. Since it's short, I'll give it to you in its entirety:

> *God be in my head, and in my understanding; God be in mine*
> *eyes, and in my looking;*
> *God be in my mouth, and in my speaking; God be in my heart,*
> *and in my thinking;*
> *God be at mine end, and at my departing.*

The lines bounce back to me now because I am struck by how much of what I've written here is about embodied knowledge: the kind of knowing that you feel in your bones, or at your fingertips or on your tongue; that is written in your heart like a promise (cross my heart and hope to die); that churns your insides or causes your central core to vibrate like a tuning fork. After the fact you remember it as a kind of prickling, or like the feel of gauzy fabric gliding over sensitized skin. This knowing is practically alive.

I am not a religious person. In fact, I lean strongly toward atheism. So what I'm referring to here as living knowledge has nothing to do with the spirit of God—even if the line that originally inspired Davies's incantatory hymn to embodiment comes from I Corinthians 3:16: "Do you not know that you are God's temple and that God's spirit dwells in you?" Which line is the source of the modern "wellness" dictum, although that dumbed-down version of the idea seems to apply uniquely to diet and toxic intake.

The embodied knowledge I'm talking about—the kind that imprints itself on the body, inside and out—more closely resembles the "minded-body" or "embodied-mind" that philosophers talk about by way of realigning for us the locus of consciousness. Think about the mystery of touch-typing, where you can distinguish mere habit from a kind of "knowledge in the hands." Technically this knowledge of where to put which fingers, and in what order, is in the head and is more commonly known as proprioception (the same ability that allows you to touch the tip of your nose with your finger when your eyes are closed). In cognitive science, proprioception is tied up with the concept of procedural memory, which explains the way we process spatial relationships and abstract patterns, and which allows us, for example, to play a Mozart sonata on the piano without even thinking about it. Or to never forget how to ride a bicycle. Although it is a truism to say you never forget how to ride a bicycle, perhaps it is more accurate to say that it is the minded-body that does the remembering. Either way, the point is it feels as if the hands know. Or the legs know.

Over the period that I have been writing this book, I've come to feel that our experience of aging is a form of embodied knowledge, which is why our bodies seem to perceive and feel and sensitize us to the changes that age brings long before our minds catch up.

We carry age in our bodies. In turn, our bodies register the subtlest of midlife shifts: an imperceptible dulling of sight or hearing, a barely noticeable decline in the number of neurons firing or in the strength of firing, a measure more of tiredness, an ever-so-gradual slowing, and so on. These subtle changes recalibrate the way we perceive and experience the world, but also, I would argue, they change the shape of our thoughts.

Aging, in other words, is psychosomatic. It is felt (understood!) in both locales. I have always had a knee-jerk distaste for the idea that age is all in the mind, and in some ways this book is an extended argument in countering that notion, bringing the body back into the frame at every turn: organs, hormones, skin, guts, muscle, heart, teeth, head, a litany of body parts that, I hope, add up to a whole. Perhaps this "embodiedness" of aging becomes increasingly constitutive of our individual identities as we travel from forty to fifty to sixty, and beyond. For my part, I'm convinced that it is not possible to fully appreciate what it means to age without attending to what the body knows.

Another problem (take note, defenders of "age is all in the mind"): the thing about embodied knowledge is that as soon as you try to consciously control it, you end up hampering the process. I've experienced this kind of arrest playing the piano, when I've consciously tried thinking, mid-sonata, *What comes next?*—only to find that my hands instantly seize up. They can't play a note. There is a lesson in this for how we age. We have to let our bodies do it for us. Our minds will either check out—the developmental equivalent of your hands seizing up—or they will process what has happened after the fact. We will have performed aging regardless of whether we choose to applaud it or walk out of the theater.

The French philosopher Maurice Merleau-Ponty was fascinated by the idea of "being-in-the-world"—the words all linked up because he thought that you cannot separate being from knowing. He marveled at the way human consciousness is incarnate. His thesis, if you like, deeply pagan, is that the body itself is a form of consciousness.

According to Merleau-Ponty, bodily consciousness underpins many states and activities we tend to think of as mental, such as believing, desiring, or thinking. It is equally manifest in the act of perception and in our (often unconscious) deliberations around acting. We apprehend our environment, for instance, not as some passive external thing, but as something that "invites" us to interact with it, "offering" certain possibilities for action and "disallowing" others. We might sense the city by night to be forbidding, or a vista of green fields quilting the hills to be beckoning or uplifting. We sense that some dogs are not-to-be-stroked, that certain foods look appetizing. Perception, in other words, has an affective or emotive component that is *felt*; and such feelings, in turn, determine how we comport ourselves and what behavior we judge appropriate.

When people talk glibly about age-appropriate behavior, they tend to overlook the very real, sensory dimension of affectiveness that is in play. It is my body that tells me that I don't think that bungee jumping off a tall building is a good idea at my age. Whether I listen is a different matter. It is my body that tells me when I've been out in the sun for too long, or when I've had too much to drink, when I've spent too many hours online, or in a particular chair, or when I would benefit from a stretch, a walk, time with the dog, a sugary treat, a chat with a friend, a different order of task (editing to cut up the writing, cleaning the house to better let my unconscious brain do its work). Stored up, learned and cherished, this is a kind of knowing that signifies maturity. The academic expositors of Merleau-Ponty have a neat term for this knowledge: they call it absorbed coping.

Absorbed coping is such a suggestive phrase, not least because of its immediate and vernacular appeal: it simply makes good sense. But if we transpose the idea across from philosophy to neuroscience, we arrive at something not so different from the feedback loop; that is, the way neural pathways respond to environmental challenges by becoming increasingly defined and effective over time, like chiseling a groove into a piece of hardwood.

As our experiences of the world accrete, they change us. As ever, it is Colette who has given me food for thought on this theme. Colette once likened her aging self to a tempered steed, "sharpened and hardened" by her sufferings. When, at thirty-six, she discerned the first "claw marks" of age, they pierced her to her core, precisely because she was able to see beyond them to the "elastic," "velvety," and "rosy girl" now gone forever. "You have to get old," she told herself then, following this up with a mantra-like injunction: "Repeat the words to yourself, not as a howl of despair but as the boarding call to a necessary departure."

Colette lived by her body, by its rhythms and modes. She cleaved to its appetites—which some might see as a weakness—but also relished the lessons it taught her. Her determination to keep fit, to acquire a "modern" body, to sculpt her muscles (whose true beauty, says her biographer Judith Thurman, was identical with their purpose, which was self-support), was a way of sharpening her senses, but also her resolve. Her passion for dance and gymnastics was no less spiritual than physical in origin and expression: "When my body thinks, all my flesh has a soul," she wrote in *The Retreat from Love* (1907). I love the pagan twist Colette gives the idea of the sacred body, and when I think of her writing these words, I picture her at peace with herself. Lit up from within, bathed in a numinous glow.

Although she did not find aging agreeable, Colette tackled it with characteristic gusto. She was a mistress of absorbed coping. Experiencing a terrific burst of energy in her fifties, she went with the direction of flow, throwing herself into writing, touring plays, traveling, and exploring new loves. Then in 1932, at the age of fifty-nine, per-haps foreseeing that soon she'd no longer be capable of outrunning time, she did the oddest thing: she masked her slowing down with a compensatory quickening. She opened a beauty business. She raised 750,000 francs, refurbished an old salon with art deco mir-rors and chrome fittings and evolved a range of high-end creams and makeup products (based on her Burgundian home recipes) that were sold in chic little black pots. She told the world she was "resting" from writing. And the world—or at least *le tout Paris*—flocked to her door on the rue Miromesnil, jockeying for a turn in the black leather chair where the great writer, dressed in a white lab coat, performed makeovers.

Needless to say, the business did not last: expanding too quickly into Saint-Tropez, then Nantes, it collapsed within a year, under the pressure of its own overzealous optimism. Thankfully for us, Colette decided that writing and aging made for better bedfellows than aging and entrepreneurialism.

"When my body thinks . . . ," wrote Colette. The words are so simple, but the meaning so profound. I think that I have always understood these words. It is why I take myself for a walk when I want to engage my brain, and why I feel euphoric when I run. It is why I've always held the conviction that people who love their food also love being alive: it's not about blind consumption, it's about taste (and that complicated link between savor and dis-cernment). It is also why I dedicated myself to ballet throughout my childhood. Though I would never have expressed it this way if you had asked me at the time, I found concentrating on the preci-sion and poise that ballet demanded of me intrinsically centering. When my fingers and arms traced the right kind of arcing lines, or when my spine was rod straight as I dunked it into a plié, I felt somehow at home in myself. Then there is that wondrous sense of gathering, of strength and of purpose that arrives with adolescence, tautening like a powerful limb as you grow into yourself. My daughter has arrived at this juncture. I see it in the way she moves, and I watch her with delight.

Recently, I've had to learn a bit of absorbed coping myself. I have developed a more or less continual pain in my hip, which keeps me awake at night and which is currently mystifying my doctors. (I've been bounced from neurologists to rheumatologists to surgeons to radiologists, without any definitive diagnosis.) What is clear, however, is that I've got a bulging disk between two of the vertebrae in my lower spine (the ones compressed by scoliosis), and my facet joints—those primeval-looking structures, like tiny teeth, that link one vertebra to another—are degenerating. Squashing my nerve roots, these developments have bequeathed me sciatica.

What does it mean to live with chronic pain? And also to live inside of pain? This is a new experience for me, introducing a fresh dread to my concerns about aging, but also acquainting me with a new kind of fatalism. When I look down the lens at sixty, and seventy, and eighty, I worry that I am looking along a steep curve of escalating bodily trauma. There are medications I can take, but they tend to dull my thinking. Yet if I don't take them, how will I endure the progressive pain? These are the sorts of trade-offs that I imagine will present themselves more commonly as aging takes a firmer grip.

Once again, I marvel at my mother, whose bookkeeping talents have allowed her to offset the deficits of aging with skill: living with pain, juggling suffering with joy, bereavement with survival. These checks and balances address the question of ongoingness, the problem of balance. But then my new acquaintance with fatalism washes in, firm and true as a tide, and carries me off in another direction. At the end of the day, I am tempted to shrug my shoulders in the face of it all and say *que sera, sera*. I am learning to be cavalier. Which is just as well, since there is not a thing I can do about what aging will bring my way.

This summer I turned fifty-one. It felt like nothing. On the day itself, I came home from a week's teaching of a residential writing course so sapped of energy that I fell into the house, wilting. With a sleep deficit that matched that of any new parent and five hours on the Great Western Railway behind me, all I was good for was a stiff drink in the garden, followed by ten hours of blackout sleep. That was fine. In fact, it was more than fine. It was a blessed relief for the 5 and the 1 to not matter. I suspect, looking ahead, that sixty will not represent the enormous hurdle that fifty has thrown in my path, that I have broken the back of my fear of moving forward. Writing it out has helped. Interrogating my anxieties, my grief, my sense of loss, my nostalgia, my hauntings: all of this has been a form of exorcism. Another way of traveling lighter.

None of which is to say that my minded-body will not still ambush me on occasion, as it did that spring in Paris, when the Musée Rodin was the unwitting trigger. Such invisible tripwires abound. I stumble on them when I find myself inexplicably overlooked—literally not seen—when in mixed company and there are women present, younger than me, drawing the available energy in a room, and leading me to feel almost molecularly insubstantial. Or when I feel energized by watching street dancers and my limbs are eager, so eager, to attempt those impossible moves. Or again, when I'm striding down the high street on some errand or other, and I unwittingly glimpse myself in a shop-front mirror and momentarily experience that heart-stopping dissonance between what I see and what I didn't even realize I had expected to see. The strangeness of the reflected image floors me every time, like being spooked by your own shadow. Or, more accurately, visited by a ghost from the future. I try to picture myself at sixty. It's not that hard, since my mother got there before me and with each passing year I grow more like her (while she, in turn, reminds me more and more of my grandmother, who was not much younger than my mother is now when I was a child). I can see that I'll look more Iraqi as time works its effects—payback for all that youthful double-speed pedaling away from my roots. Will my daughter join the queue? It seems inevitable. It makes me smile to visualize the succession, because to me the flow of movement is clear, and it's not top-down, the way my mother with her baton-handing notions sees it. What I see instead is one of those penny-pushing machines you find in old-fashioned arcades at British seaside towns: you toss a bright new coin into the slot, hoping that when it hits the tray beneath—heaped with old coppers—it will generate enough of a shove to tip a few of the old-timers over the cliff edge, falling noisily into the gutter below.

The funny thing is I don't mind the shove. I no longer want what I used to want. And now that I've lost my fear of forward motion, I won't be wasting my energies treading water, puffing and struggling to stay in the same place, forever battling time and attempting to outwit mirrors.

Epilogue

LOOKING OUT MY STUDY WINDOW, HIGH UP AMID THE TREETOPS, I peer through a blizzard of leaves shaped like splayed hands and watch my daughter walk the dog around the outside rim of the square. They make a grand sight: her in denim shorts and jacket, ponytail swishing behind her in time with her feet, him a fluff ball with a honey-colored pom-pom tail. With an officious air, the dog trots along ahead of her on short legs, thinking that he is walking her. She doesn't mind. When he's done pulling her along, she takes him into the square and sits down on the benches next to one of the young mums. She knows them all, can tell me who lives where. She'll be there awhile, I suspect, chatting away, talking about the challenges of her friendship group at school, the favorite teacher who lives nearby in Dalston, the music she likes to listen to, the ice-skating competition she's just signed up for where she's got to do a salchow and a three jump. Later, when I look out, she's showing them the moves: the upright spins, the graceful arabesques. She's like a healthy plant reaching for the sun. Not for the first time my heart swells watching her. It fills my chest and climbs up into my mouth so that I can't talk.

Although it is high summer and the square is a pointillist vision of emerald and forest greens, it is not as wild as it used to be. Last year the local council in its bureaucratic wisdom, head turned by Austerity, decided that Wilton Square had to be reined in. All that excess and profusion—all that fecundity—seemed to have given offense, as though it were too ostentatious a show of wealth amid Britain's recent economic impoverishment. It had to go.

A team of landscape gardeners was sent in to tackle the overgrowth. Like ground forces on a vital mission, they disappeared into its midst to claw back bushes and hedgerows from the inside out, while council vehicles in the street shredded plant matter all day long, as if hiding the evidence. One day the railings reappeared. Then the brightly colored doors belonging to the houses opposite became visible. One evening, returning home from work, I was stopped dead in my tracks because so many of the flowering trees had simply gone. My heart fell to the floor. Whether they'd been cut down or pulled out, I couldn't tell, and in any case the effect was the same: it was awful. Like a gaping mouth that had lost most of its teeth to rot, the square looked disfigured.

The following week the council scaled up its offensive and sent in a highly professional team of aerialists who made it look as though the plane trees had been suddenly occupied by a troupe of circus performers. They swung from arbor to arbor with deftness and flair, suspended in harnesses and with chain saws hanging at eye-watering angles, attached to belts at their waists. Watching them was mesmerizing. You'd glimpse their bright yellow construction hats through the leaves. Hear them shout over the grinding buzz of the sawing and watch heavy branches come crashing down. At each wholesale felling, the tree surgeons whooped and called. Then they'd all swing to the next branch over, threading and clipping ropes as they flew. And then the unthinkable happened: one of the tree surgeons fell. Presumably he sawed through his safety rope, but he plummeted sixty feet and impaled himself on the railing below in the horrific manner made infamous by Vlad Dracula. I wasn't home, but my husband said the man's cry was something he would never forget—a deep and tortured animal moan. It didn't last long because the poor man passed out almost immediately. When I got back, I found the road cordoned off by police, yellow tape zigzagging everywhere, and three ambulances were still parked in the square. The fourth had already left, carrying the doctors who had had to gingerly pluck their patient, slumped unconscious, off the spike.

The next day a mournful silence hung over Wilton Square. All activities had been suspended. Residents went about their business quietly, not knowing if the tree surgeon had made it. Then a few days later work was resumed. There was no whooping. I asked one of the men about his colleague. He had lived, I was told. I gulped in relief. But it had been touch and go for a few hours as surgeons had tried to mend the internal damage. "Luckily none of his arteries was punctured," said the tree surgeon, "so he's gonna pull through. Thing is, if he'd landed on the road from that height, he'd have died. No question." Landing on the spike, then, had perversely saved him. The wound, the injury, the unbelievable pain he'd endured, had been his good fortune.

It took a long time for me to see the square properly after that. It was as if the whole place had sucked up a sharp intake of breath and then not exhaled it. There was a feeling of tension, of something being held in, of difficulty and discomfort. I walked about with that somatic knifing feeling stabbing my groin whenever I thought of the injured man—and I thought of him every time I gazed up at the leafy canopy. I went to the spot where he'd fallen, not really knowing what I was looking for, but naturally there was nothing to see. I wondered at his incredible bad luck—and then his good luck, and then at life's ridiculous turns. I thought about how certain events seem to pick you out and chase you down, forcing you to underscore your life into Before and After. They are seismic. They shift the world. And sometimes they alter the atmosphere itself. But still we cope, and we survive them.

One year on, and with the mothers and dog walkers and teenagers now returned, with life washing back in over the ground soil of trauma, some kind of normality has been resumed. We have a new square now, city-tame but austerely beautiful, trimmed down and elegantly restrained. Neat miniature rosebushes have been planted where the smaller trees used to be, and lavender bushes encircle the central benches. In summer they smell divine. Instead of a wall of green confronting you when you walk into the square, you get a wonderfully modulated view: the plane trees are still standout gorgeous, but now the pared-back greenery below allows the light and the breeze to play among the leaves, and you can pick out a motley of different-colored flowers amid the vegetal flutter and shimmer. Slowly, I am learning to appreciate the square's sharper contours, its pared-down form. It has a softer footprint now and a new lightness of being.

Notes

8 The Museum of Modern Art in New York mounted an exhibition of Nicholas Nixon's photographs of the Brown sisters at the end of 2014. *Forty Years of the Brown Sisters* attracted international coverage, and *The New York Times Magazine* allowed readers to access the entire series of images here: http://www.nytimes.com/interactive/2014/10/03/magazine/01-brown-sisters-forty-years.html. These pictures sit nicely inside the photographer's wider oeuvre. Nixon works almost exclusively in black and white, and his photographic studies include many portraits of the very old and very young, the sick and dying and the blinking newborn, often juxtaposing infant and geriatric subjects in the same shot. Time, generation, loss, these are Nixon's themes. They are everyday themes, but his pictures give them a monumental weight.

11 Whether or not the andropause, or in popular coinage "manopause," is real is not a question that concerns biology, since in endocrine terms there is no male equivalent of menopause: no end of fertility, no hormonal cessation. But of course in publishing terms it is a *thing*—a phenomenon that can be blown up into a popular book. Hence we have *The Andropause Mystery: Unraveling Truths about the Male Menopause*, by Robert S. Tan, MD (Amred Publishing, 2009), for example, or Jed Diamond's *Male Menopause* (Sourcebooks, 1997), with a "Foreword by John Gray, PhD." Note the flagging up of academic credentials on the dust jacket, a practice that generally arouses the suspicion that what's between the covers must be contentious—the very opposite of what the showy qualifications are intended to convey.

14 Simone de Beauvoir's *La Vieillesse* was published by Gallimard in 1970, when de Beauvoir was sixty-two, appearing two years later in English as *The Coming of Age* (G. P. Putnam's Sons, 1972). "Society looks upon old age as a kind of shameful secret that it is unseemly to mention. . . . I mean to break the conspiracy of silence," wrote de Beauvoir in the introduction. The book is encyclopedic in its scope and endlessly fascinating. De Beauvoir explores aging through the specialisms of history, anthropology, philosophy, literature, and science, sprinkling her prose with rich anecdotes and literary quotations. One of the most arresting passages for me is where de Beauvoir, over the space of almost three pages (pp. 25–27), simply lists everything that happens to the human body as it ages, from the cellular level outward. Lately, Lynne Segal has written at length about de Beauvoir's writing on aging, both in *The Coming of Age* and elsewhere. Her book *Out of Time: The Pleasures and Perils of Ageing* (Verso, 2013) weighs how feminists have fared through the second half of the twentieth century in redefining cultural attitudes toward aging.

26–29 Christiane Northrup, *The Wisdom of Menopause: The Complete Guide to Physical and Emotional Health During the Change* (Piatkus, 2001). Quotations are from pp. 2, 3, 6, 9, 43, and 361. These days Northrup is a one-woman inspiration industry: after following up *Wisdom* with *The Secret Pleasures of Menopause* (Hay House, 2008), her latest offering is aimed at women "seniors" determined to do more with their lives than give themselves up to being serene: *Goddesses Never Age: The Secret Prescription for Radiance, Vitality, and Well-being* (Hay House, 2015).

29–30 Jaki Scarcello, *Fifty & Fabulous!: The Best Years of a Woman's Life* (Watkins Publishing, 2010). Quotations are from pp. 38, 67, and passim. The work on gerotranscendence that Scarcello repeatedly cites, and that rises far above her own book in credibility and standing, is Lars Tornstam's *Gerotranscendence: A Developmental Theory of Positive Aging* (Springer Publishing Company, 2005).

31 I'll not be thanked by the feminist authors I cite here for calling out their books as works I found difficult to get on with, and certainly their work spurred me to develop my own take on menopause and midlife; but in their own ways both Angela Neustatter's *The Year I Turn . . . : A Quirky A–Z of Ageing* (Gibson Square Books, 2014) and Anne Karpf's *How to Age* (The School of Life series, Macmillan, 2014) bear the fingerprints of positive thinking and self-actualization.

37–38 *Our Bodies, Ourselves*, by the Boston Women's Health Book Collective, was first published by the New England Free Press in 1970. I was among that generation of women who used it to learn more about their own genital anatomy as well as the various infectious diseases that sexually active women might be prone to develop. No matter how well informed I was on these health matters, the hospital doctor treating me for the pelvic inflammatory disease I developed at twenty-three still felt free to tell me that I ought to "keep my dignity" when I suggested that he examine me.

Nicole Ostrow's report for Bloomberg about the links between Premarin and women developing blood clots can be found here: http://www.bloomberg.com/news/articles/2013-09-30/pfizer-s-premarin-for-menopause-linked-to-blood-clot-risk

40–41 I've quoted liberally from "The Fate of the Nontreated Post-menopausal Woman: A Plea for the Maintenance of Adequate Estrogen from Puberty to the Grave," by Robert A. Wilson and Thelma A. Wilson, *Journal of the American Geriatrics Society* 11 (April 1963): 347–62.

41–42 Robert A. Wilson, *Feminine Forever* (M. Evans and Company, 1966). My quotations are from the introduction. In my reading around the history of HRT, I consulted several books; the best of them was Sheila M. Rothman and David J. Rothman's *The Pursuit of Perfection: The Promise and Perils of Medical Enhancement* (Pantheon Books, 2003)—it is in this book that Edmund Novak's disagreements with Wilson are detailed. Judith A. Houck's *Hot and Bothered: Women,*

Medicine, and Menopause in Modern America (Harvard University Press, 2006) is both detailed and entertaining. See also Elizabeth Siegel Watkins, *The Estrogen Elixir: A History of Hormone Replacement Therapy in America* (Johns Hopkins University Press, 2007).

46 Amanda Melpolder, Amy Widman, and Joanne Doroshow, "The Bitterest Pill: How Drug Companies Fail to Protect Women and How Lawsuits Save Their Lives," a report published by the Center for Justice & Democracy in 2008.

46–49 Ronald Wilson's confessions appeared in Rebecca Goldsmith's article "Advocate's Son Feared Dangers of Hormones" in New Jersey's *Star-Ledger*, July 13, 2002.

56–57 *Cosmopolitan* magazine's tribute to the maturity of the middle-aged woman is cited in Patricia Cohen's *In Our Prime: The Invention of Middle Age* (Scribner, 2012), p. 33. Cohen's lively and erudite book attempts a kind of biography of an idea: middle age. Mostly it is a social history of the subject, from the mid-nineteenth century to the present day, but Cohen augments this history with long detours through science and psychology. Her basic argument is that middle age is a "malleable cultural fiction," and her book charts how our concepts of middle age have varied with each successive generation, as society, cultural values, and medical knowledge have shifted to give women more freedom, and the middle-aged in general, more power. It's a book whose upswing—never has middle age looked better or been in better health—mirrors that of the baby boomers.

The quotation from *Lolly Willowes, or The Loving Huntsman* (1926) comes from Maroula Joannou, "'Nothing Is Impracticable for a Single, Middle-Aged Woman with an Income of Her Own': The Spinster in Women's Fiction of the 1920s," in *This Working-Day World: Women's Lives and Culture(s) in Britain, 1914–1945*, edited by Sybil Oldfield (Taylor & Francis, 1994), pp. 175–91. These paragraphs about women's newfound sense of entitlement also draw on Kay Heath's *Aging by the*

Book: The Emergence of Midlife in Victorian Britain (State University of New York Press, 2009) and Kathleen Woodward's *Ageing and Its Discontents: Freud and Other Fictions* (Indiana University Press, 1991).

57–58 Frederick Winslow Taylor, *The Principles of Scientific Management* (Harper & Brothers, 1911). Quotation is from the introduction. For background on Taylor, see Robert Kanigel's *The One Best Way: Frederick Winslow Taylor and the Enigma of Efficiency* (Viking Press, 1997).

58 Age as a "proxy for efficiency," in Patricia Cohen, p. 50.

60–61 Cheryl Miller offers a reading of *Twilight Sleep* from the perspective of the history of science and identifies the real-life sources of some of Wharton's characters. The Mahatma, for example, with his hip-slimming exercises and "mental deep-breathing," is most likely based on the popular yogi and founder of the Self-Realization Fellowship, Paramahansa Yogananda. An Indian-born seeker and later a seer, he lectured at Carnegie Hall in NYC in the 1920s on subjects such as "Everlasting Youth: Psycho-Physiological Rejuvenation of Cells by Recharging the Body Battery." Pauline Manford's next guru, Alvah Loft, master of "Spiritual Vacuum-Cleaning" (to which Pauline submits in order to have her frustrations removed "as if they'd been adenoids"), would meanwhile have sat very comfortably inside the pages of Emile Coué's 1922 bestseller, *Self Mastery Through Conscious Autosuggestion*, a book primarily remembered today for its deservedly maligned mantra: "Every day, in every respect, I am getting better and better." See Cheryl Miller, "The Painless Peace of *Twilight Sleep*," in *The New Atlantis* 18 (Fall 2007): 99–106.

61 Edith Wharton, *Twilight Sleep* (Virago Modern Classics, 1996). This edition has a short, insightful introduction by Penelope Farmer.

67–68 More on the human talent for facial recognition can be found in Vicki Bruce and Andy Young's "Understanding Face Recognition," in the *British Journal of Psychology* 77, no. 3 (August 1986): 305–27, and

Kamran Etemad and Rama Chellappa's article "Discriminant Analysis for Recognition of Human Face Images," in the *Journal of the Optical Society of America A* 14, no. 8 (1997): 1724–33.

68 Claudia Hammond, *Time Warped: Unlocking the Mysteries of Time Perception* (Canongate, 2012). This is popular science rather than the cutting-edge kind—but with appreciable gains in clarity for every loss of specialist detail. A good armchair read.

74 Basil Bunting's epic seven-hundred-line poem, "Briggflatts," was first published in 1965. The lines I've quoted are from Part 1. The poem is reprinted in *Complete Poems*, edited by Richard Caddel (Oxford University Press, 1994).

75 What makes a "good death"? Far and away the best cultural history of our attitudes to death and dying in the West is Philippe Ariès's seminal study *The Hour of Our Death* (Penguin, 1981). For a more specific history of the *ars moriendi* there's Mary Catherine O'Connor's *The Art of Dying Well: The Development of the Ars Moriendi*, 1942 (AMS Press, 1966).

79–80 Carl Jung's "The Stages of Life" was originally published in German in 1930 and was translated by W. S. Dell and Cary F. Baynes, in *Modern Man in Search of a Soul* (Routledge & Kegan Paul, 1933). It is reprinted in *The Collected Works of C. G. Jung*, edited by Sir Herbert Read, Michael Fordham, Gerhard Adler, and William McGuire (Routledge & Kegan Paul, 1972), vol. 8, pp. 387–403. Quotations from pp. 397, 399, and 400. A book-length treatment of Jung's thinking about middle age can be found in Murray Stein's *In Midlife: A Jungian Perspective*, 1983 (Chiron Publications, 2014). I also consulted Jung's various papers on "Psychological Types," in the abovementioned *Collected Works* (1971), vol. 6, pp. 497–542.

82 Carl Jung, *Memories, Dreams, Reflections*, recorded and edited by Aniela Jaffé (1963). I used the Fontana Library of Theology and

Philosophy edition (1967). My initial quotation is from the prologue. The rest of the quotations come from the chapter titled "Confrontation with the Unconscious." So much has been written about Jung that I thought I'd pick two interpretive books that I found useful: a thoughtful "primer" edited by Polly Young-Eisendrath and Terence Dawson, called *The Cambridge Companion to Jung*, 2nd ed. (Cambridge University Press, 2008), and Andrew Samuels's highly readable *Jung and the Post-Jungians* (Routledge & Kegan Paul, 1985).

84 The classic account of liminality is Victor Turner's, written up in various books, notably "Betwixt and Between: The Liminal Period in *Rites de Passage*," in *The Forest of Symbols: Aspects of Ndembu Ritual* (Cornell University Press, 1967), pp. 93–111. Here Turner describes liminality as a "fruitful darkness," saying, "Liminality is the realm of primitive hypothesis, where there is a certain freedom to juggle with the factors of existence. As in the works of Rabelais, there is a promiscuous intermingling and juxtaposing of the categories of event, experience, and knowledge, with a pedagogic intention" (p. 106). A more extensive account of liminality is given in Turner's *The Ritual Process: Structure and Anti-Structure* (Aldine Books, 1969). See chapters 3 and 5.

94 Mirroring in psychoanalytic parlance is a form of transference. An exception is Lacan's concept of the "mirror stage," which is a critical stage of self-identity formation. It is generally discussed in the specialist literature in regard to infancy and the development of a self. For more background and theory on mother-daughter mirroring, which more closely belongs in the transference category, a good place to begin is with Marianne Hirsch, *The Mother/Daughter Plot: Narrative, Psychoanalysis, Feminism* (Indiana University Press, 1989).

95 Suzanne Braun Levine, *The Woman's Guide to Second Adulthood: Inventing the Rest of Our Lives* (Bloomsbury, 2005). Like Christiane Northrup, Levine has become something of a one-woman industry, churning out high-end self-help books, delivering TED Talks, and preaching self-acceptance. The title of her recent book says it all: *Fifty Is the New Fifty* (2009).

96 The quotations about Vienna's harboring a "Paulinian" atmosphere and Joan Erikson shouting, "We left ourselves out," are in Lawrence J. Friedman's *Identity's Architect: A Biography of Erik H. Erikson* (Free Association Books, 1999), pp. 60 and 218.

Erikson introduced his staged model of identity development in his book *Childhood and Society* (1950), but its more fully articulated form appeared in *Identity and the Life Cycle* (1959) and in *The Life Cycle Completed* (1982), a book Erik cowrote with Joan. An expanded version of this book was released in 1998 (a year after Joan died, aged ninety-four). It contained an extra chapter written by her, outlining a ninth developmental stage, representing extreme old age, that she had added when she was in her nineties. See pp. 105–14. The psychic tension in this phase of life is between "Integrity" and "Despair and Disgust," and its associated virtue is "Wisdom." My quotations about generativity versus intimacy, etc., come from *The Life Cycle Completed, Extended Version* (Norton, 1998), pp. 67 and 70.

99 Francine Benes's paper—the first of several she published on the subject—is (cowritten with M. Turtle, Y. Khan, and P. Farol) "Myelination of a Key Relay Zone in the Hippocampal Formation Occurs in the Human Brain During Childhood, Adolescence and Adulthood," *Archives of General Psychiatry* 51, no. 6 (June 1994): 477–84.

"The Wonders of the Middle-Aged Brain," which summarizes the latest neuroscientific findings in the field, takes up the entirety of *On the Brain*, the newsletter published by the Harvard Mahoney Neuroscience Institute, vol. 19, no. 3 (Fall 2013). For a fuller treatment of the subject see Schahram Akbarian and Farah Lubin, eds., *Epigenetics and Neuroplasticity: Evidence and Debate*, vol. 128 in the series *Progress in Molecular Biology and Translational Science* (Elsevier Science Publishing, 2014).

102-3 Take a look at Balzac's head for yourself, here: http://www
.musee-rodin.fr/en/collections/ceramics/monumental-head-balzac.
As for Stendhal's syndrome, all you need to know about it, in my view,
can be found in Iain Bamforth's lively article "Stendhal's Syndrome," in
British Journal of General Practice 60, no. 581 (December 2010): 945–46.
(British Library readers can access it online.)

104-5 My source for Everett's ideas is Peter Byrne's article "The Many
Worlds of Hugh Everett," in *Scientific American* 297, no. 6 (December
2007): 72–79. To situate many worlds in the hotly debated context of
actual physics, see Philip Ball, "Is the Many Worlds Hypothesis Just a
Fantasy?" *Aeon*, February 17, 2015.

110-11 I became fascinated with the subject of menopause in whales
after reading an article called "Killer Whales, Grandmas and What
Men Want: Evolutionary Biologists Consider Menopause," in *Science
News*, August 19, 2013. While numerous articles have been published
about menopause in orcas over the past couple of decades, the extent
to which the whales exhibit any symptomatology remains extremely
unclear. What behavioral information marine scientists do have
on female orcas, however, has been used to support and refine our
understanding of evolutionary biology in higher mammals. Many
of the articles I read are available online. See Eric J. Ward, Elizabeth F. Holmes, and Ken C. Balcomb, "Quantifying the Effects of
Prey Abundance on Killer Whale Reproduction," *Journal of Applied
Ecology* 46 (2009): 632–40; Emma A. Foster et al., "Adaptive Prolonged Postreproductive Life Span in Killer Whales," *Science* 337, no.
6100 (September 14, 2012): 1313; and Lauren J. N. Brent et al., "Eco-
logical Knowledge, Leadership and the Evolution of Menopause in
Killer Whales," *Current Biology* 26, no. 6 (March 2015): 746–50. For an
armchair read there's also Hal Whitehead and Luke Rendell's highly
readable book, *The Cultural Lives of Whales and Dolphins* (University
of Chicago Press, 2014).

111 K- and R-strategists are two of the life-history strategists characterized by the American ecologist Robert MacArthur and evolutionary biologist E. O. Wilson. K-selected species are those whose populations fluctuate at or near the carrying capacity (k) of the environment in which they reside. R-selected species are those whose populations are governed by their biotic potential or maximum reproductive capacity (r).

112 George C. Williams's paper on the "grandmother hypothesis" is "Pleiotropy, Natural Selection and the Evolution of Senescence," in *Evolution* 11, no. 4 (1957): 398–411.

112–13 See K. Hawkes, J. F. O'Connell, and N. G. Blurton Jones, "Hadza Women's Time Allocation, Offspring Provisioning and the Evolution of Long Postmenopausal Life Spans," in *Current Anthropology* 38, no. 4 (1997): 551–77.

115 Margaret Mead first talked about "postmenopausal zestfulness" in an interview for *Life* magazine in 1959. See Nancy Lutkehaus, *Margaret Mead: The Making of an American Icon* (Princeton University Press, 2008), p. 73.

118 Between them Greer and Sheehy put menopause on the map and made it something women could both write and talk about. Germaine Greer's *The Change: Women, Ageing and the Menopause* (Hamish Hamilton, 1991) to my mind remains the baldest and most gutsy account of menopause to date. It's full of literary references and personal insight and political pique. Gail Sheehy's *The Silent Passage: Menopause* (Random House, 1992) was an all-out blockbuster. Pacy and anecdotal, rather than rigorous and revealing, it dishes up a smorgasbord of female menopausal experience.

119–20 The book that will guide you around the hocus-pocus that passes for math in longevity studies is S. Jay Olshansky and Bruce A. Carnes's *The Quest for Immortality: Science at the Frontiers of Aging*

(Norton, 2001). Olshansky, a professor in the School of Public Health at the University of Chicago, and Carnes work at the same university's Center on Aging. They are very strong on how statistics are routinely misread and therefore misused, and also good at peeling away the folklore, cryptoscience, and false reasoning around how and why people age. What makes Michael Rose so compelling, meanwhile, is that he's a convert. Having successfully extended the lives of fruit flies by selectively breeding only those flies that reproduced most late in their life cycle, and finding that several generations down the line the fruit flies that were thus bred lived measurably longer than their peers, Rose has begun to see the limits of genomics. See, for example, "Adaptation, Aging, and Genomic Information," in *Aging* 1, no. 5 (May 2009): 444–50.

126 I wrote up my trip to Baghdad as part of a book-length family history that novelized the life of my grandmother and offered a portrait of a community that at one point exemplified Iraq's commitment to an early (1920s and '30s) experiment in multiculturalism, but which was then tragically sacrificed to the realpolitik of the mid-twentieth century. See *Last Days in Babylon: The Story of the Jews of Iraq* (Bloomsbury, 2007).

127–28 Judith Thurman's *Secrets of the Flesh: A Life of Colette* (Bloomsbury, 1999) is simply the best biography of Colette available in English. I've leaned on it shamelessly in this chapter, but readers who might not want to commit to a full six-hundred-page life will find a summary biography and plenty else to mull over in Angela Carter's wonderful essay "Colette," published in the *London Review of Books* 2, no. 19 (October 2, 1980): 15–17 (available online).

129 Colette, *Break of Day* (Capuchin Classics, 2012). This edition has a terrific introduction by the journalist Lisa Allardice, who is impishly amused by imagining "how Colette would laugh!" at the "improving" literature of today—"the self-help titles claiming to empower women, extolling us to love ourselves, seize the day and stand on our own two feet," p. 12.

134 Simone de Beauvoir, *The Coming of Age*, p. 11.

135–38 Maurice Goudeket, *Close to Colette*, translated by Enid McLeod (Secker & Warburg, 1957). Goudeket describes life at La Treille Muscate on pp. 33–40. I've quoted from pp. 4, 39, and 51. There's a lovely description here, I suspect hammed up a little by Goudeket, of how Colette would explore flowers she encountered in any new garden. He says, "It was not enough to look at them, she had to sniff and taste them. When she went into a garden she did not know, I would say: 'I suppose you're going to eat it, as usual.' And it was extraordinary to see her setting to work, full of haste and eagerness, as if there were no more urgent task than getting to know this garden. She separated the sepals of flowers, examined them, smelled them for a long time, crumpled the leaves, chewed them, licked the poisonous berries and the deadly mushrooms, pondering intensely over everything she had smelt and tasted. Insects received almost the same treatment: they were felt and listened to and questioned." At the end of this, "with her nose and her forehead covered with yellow pollen, her hair in disorder and full of twigs, a bump here and a scratch there, her face innocent of powder and her neck moist, stumbling along out of breath . . . she was just like a bacchante after libations," p. 15.

136 Thomas Merton's "A Practical Program for Monks" is reprinted in *The Collected Poems of Thomas Merton* (Sheldon Press, 1978), pp. 797–99.

147–48 Kirsty Milne, *At Vanity Fair: From Bunyan to Thackeray* (Cambridge University Press, 2015).

157 There is no better meditation on the poetics of ritual and its association to circular time than Mircea Eliade's classic study of 1955, *Cosmos and History: The Myth of the Eternal Return* (Garland, 1985).

158 John Bunyan and Robert Southey, *The Pilgrim's Progress, with a Life of John Bunyan* (John Murray, 1830); the passage about Christian and Hopeful fording the river is on pp. 204–6.

161 Laurence Binyon, "The Burning of the Leaves," in *The Burning of the Leaves and Other Poems*, edited by Cicely Margaret Binyon (Macmillan, 1944).

166–67 An excellent introduction to the work and thought of Maurice Merleau-Ponty can be found on the *IEP*, or *Internet Encyclopedia of Philosophy*: http://www.iep.utm.edu/merleau/. Shogo Tanaka's blog, http://embodiedknowledge.blogspot.co.uk/, is also helpful for making connections between philosophical thinking on the subject and more scientific explanations. For Merleau-Ponty on touch-typing, see *The Phenomenology of Perception* (1945), translated by Colin Smith (Routledge Classics, 2002), p. 166. The relevant chapter is "The Spatiality of One's Own Body and Motility," which also contains fascinating discussions of "number blindness," "phantom limbs," organ playing, and more. The idea of an embodied identity is also present in psychoanalytic literature. See, for example, R. Lombardi, "Body, Affect, Thought: Reflections on the Work of Matte Blanco and Ferrari," in *Psychoanalytic Quarterly* 78, no. 1 (2009): 123–60.

167 See Komarine Romdenh-Romluc, *Merleau-Ponty and Phenomenology of Perception* (Routledge Philosophy Guidebooks, 2011). In a strict sense "absorbed coping" describes the source of our feeling at ease inside a world that offers us multiple opportunities to act, but where so many of our actions need not be thought through: how to behave at a dinner party, for example; swerving the car to avoid hitting someone; wandering into the kitchen to make a cup of tea while thinking about something else entirely. As Romdenh-Romluc writes, "Acquiring a motor skill is thus partly a matter of learning to perceive opportunities to exercise it" (p. 77). The better you become at the skill, the more opportunities to use it you're able to discern. This is true of mental as well as motor skills, implying that the more accustomed to a situation you are, the more tools you have at your disposal to offer an appropriate response. If this isn't the essence of maturity, I don't know what is.

The term *absorbed coping* was coined by Dreyfus and Dreyfus, in "The Challenge of Merleau-Ponty's Phenomenology of Embodiment for Cognitive Science," in G. Weiss and H. F. Haber, eds., *Perspectives on Embodiment: The Intersections of Nature and Culture* (Routledge, 1999). Merleau-Ponty put the matter more poetically himself, however, by referring to this environment-responsive behavior as "how to reckon with the possible." See Romdenh-Romluc, pp. 93–96.

168 Colette on the "claw marks" of aging quoted in Judith Thurman, pp. 188–89; on her desire for a "modern" body, p. 132. A wry account of the rise and fall of her beauty business is on pp. 394–96, and also in Goudeket, *Close to Colette*, pp. 59–63. "When my body thinks" is quoted by Sharyn R. Udall in *Dance and American Art: A Long Embrace* (University of Wisconsin Press, 2012), p. 95.

Acknowledgments

This book began in conversation—with friends, colleagues, my mother, my husband—all of it circling around what felt like an absence. What was this midlife crunch, this crisis, this onslaught of unwelcome change, this punch in the face, this falling, fissure, cliff-drop, or just cliff? I have Jill Chisholm and Kate Mossman to thank for spurring me into putting down my first thoughts on the subject for the *New Statesman*, which commission seeded the idea for the book—and so the conversations continued. For their impromptu input and companionship, their friendship, insight, and willingness to share with me their experiences of being no longer young, I want thank Melanie McGrath, Clare Bayley, Anne Goldgar, Greg Klerkx, Francis Spufford, Wendy Monkhouse, Victoria Finlay, Ingrid Simler, Larry Keith, Frances Barr, Katy Hazell, Tina Pepler, Katie Grant, and Marcelle Bernstein.

There are various other people I wish to thank for pointing me to useful sources, or pushing me to come up with a new thought: Kelly Boyd, Margaret Anderson, Philip Hoare, Amanda Vickery, Julia Ryde, Iain Sinclair, Andrew Samuels, Barbara Steinmetz, and Barry Bone. Greg Klerkx, Melanie McGrath, and Francis Spufford did me the invaluable service of reading early drafts of the book, and their comments and suggestions helped make it a smarter and more complex work than it would otherwise have been. An earlier version of the chapter "Heart" appeared in *Aeon* magazine in October 2014 and still bears the marks of Brigid Hains's keen editorial input. I'd also like to thank Seumas Milne and Ruairidh Milne for ensuring there were no factual errors in the chapter "Head," about their sister, Kirsty.

I wish to thank the Arts Council England for their generous support. Like moving with a tailwind, the grant for the arts they awarded me made completing the book a far more focused and speedy affair. I have also been extremely fortunate to have ongoing support from my agent, Rebecca Carter, and editor Philip Gwyn Jones. I am hugely grateful to them both for their uncompromising vision of what publishing can and ought to be doing and for giving me the freedom not just to go where my curiosity led, but also where a sense of urgency took me. They never asked me to soft-pedal the harder truths I wanted to give voice to. And if ever my spirits did flag, I could always count on Rachel Shabi and Samantha Ellis, aka the North London Iraqi-Jewish Women Writers Support Group, for a healthy dollop of encouragement.

In a climate where it has become that much more difficult to earn one's living at writing, I am grateful to the Royal Literary Fund and to Paul and Brigid Hains at Aeon Media for offering me flexible work arrangements that gave me space to write. That said, the book had a way of consuming me regardless, claiming my attention during many evenings and weekends, when I just disappeared from family life. For their forbearance and their love I want to thank my husband, Greg, and our daughter (who agreed that I could mention her in these pages providing she remained unnamed).

I have tried hard when dealing with family members and friends to stay on the right side of the mighty responsibility that comes with choosing to write personally. I am keenly aware that my story is not the only story when it comes to events and people I've documented in these pages, and that exposing myself has often entailed exposing others. This book represents only my version of things. Others who feature in it will have their own truths, which are theirs to keep or tell.

About the Author

Marina Benjamin is the author of two previous memoirs, *Rocket Dreams*, short-listed for the Eugene Emme Award, and *Last Days in Babylon*, long-listed for the Wingate Prize. She has also worked as a journalist, her pieces appearing in *The Guardian*, the *Financial Times*, *The Independent*, and other British newspapers, and she has served as arts editor at the *New Statesman* and deputy arts editor at the *Evening Standard*. She is currently a senior editor at the digital magazine *Aeon*.